JN

# CREATIVE JEWELLERY

*DINNY HALL*

# CREATIVE JEWELLERY

## DINNY HALL

EBURY PRESS
LONDON

Published by Ebury Press
Division of The National Magazine Company Ltd
Colquhoun House
27-37 Broadwick Street
London W1V 1FR

First impression 1986
Text © 1986 Dinny Hall
© 1986 The Paul Press Limited

ISBN 0 85223 585 2

Typeset by Wordsmiths, Street, Somerset
Origination by Gee & Watson. Sutton
Printed in Italy

This book was edited, designed and produced by
The Paul Press Ltd, 22 Bruton Street, London W1X 7DA

**Art Editor** Tony Paine
**Project Editor** Sally MacEachern
**Editorial** Annemarie Whittle, Emma Warlow
**Art Assistants** David Ayres, Sue Brinkhurst
**Illustrations** Hayward and Martin Ltd
**Photography** Don Wood

**Art Director** Stephen McCurdy
**Editorial Director** Jeremy Harwood
**Publishing Director** Nigel Perryman

# Contents

# Foreword

This book is dedicated to Tom Binns, with thanks for all his help, and to my mother, Susan, who has continually encouraged me.

When I decided to write **Creative Jewellery**, I started by thinking about what sort of book I would have found most useful when I started my own career. Above all, I was determined not to fall into the trap of introducing a vast mass of complicated, off-putting technical information. What I hope I have done is to combine a basic grounding in developing design ideas with sufficient practical back-up to make the art of jewellery design both approachable and rewarding. I have always considered the design of a piece of jewellery to be all-important and this is the first golden rule I would like to pass on to you. Creating an exciting design cannot depend on technical ability alone; it also needs imagination and originality. Therefore, the technical skills you should cultivate are subordinate to your design ideas – indeed I have always felt that jewellery can be made from almost anything that has a decorative purpose, has some spiritual value or expresses some point of view! Take this precept as your starting point and you will not go far wrong, irrespective of whether you are using traditional materials, such as silver, gold, base metals or gemstones, more modern ones, like plastics or titanium, or natural materials, such as bone, shell, feathers or wood. And this is why this book is centred around a core of step-by-step projects, so that you can master the techniques involved through the actual process of creation, rather than by following a sequence of inevitably abstract exercises. Each craftsman, of course, has his or her own way of doing things, as you will see from the work I have chosen as examples. I have tried to be as open-minded as possible, rather than laying down hard and fast rules, so that you can develop your own style and approach to the full. Remember, above all, that design and technical expertise are complementary and that practice will help you not only to develop all the necessary technical skills, but to select the ones most suited to the task in hand.

The keynote throughout is my belief that jewellery design should be approachable. My aim has been to show beginners with no technical knowledge, a way of obtaining the necessary skills, while showing others, perhaps with some practical experience, a range of ideas and techniques that might help to broaden their outlook. But, most of all, I hope that **Creative Jewellery** will help you to enjoy the art of jewellery design, whether you anticipate making things as a hobby or as a possible career.

# Principles of design

When you try to judge the success of a piece of jewellery —
whether it is your own work or someone else's — there are
certain questions you should ask yourself. First of all, your
own personal taste aside, does it suit the wearer? No
matter how beautiful the piece is, it will not look its best if
it does not complement the personality and physique of
the person wearing it. A large chunky ring will look heavy
on a short, chubby finger. A delicate pearl and silver
brooch will pale into insignificance on a flamboyant,
multicoloured dress.

Does the piece of jewellery work on a technical level?
Bangles must not be so tight or heavy that they are
uncomfortable to wear. Brooch pins should not come
undone or protrude to the extent of risking damaging the
material or injuring the wearer.

How original is the piece? Copies will always look like
copies. Few pieces can be totally original, but each should
have some individual quality which reflects the
personality of the designer.

Regardless of whether you are assessing a piece of fine
jewellery, costume jewellery, fashion jewellery or
theatrical jewellery, your final opinion must take into
account whether the potential of the materials used has
been explored to the full. The most successful and
memorable pieces of work harmoniously link the design of
the piece with the materials used; colour, texture, shape
and proportion all combining to form a pleasing whole.

While it is probably true that some people are born with
more talent than others and that design originality cannot
be taught, it is quite possible for anyone to learn how to
produce attractive and individual jewellery. Even if you
see yourself as unartistic you will find that, by studying
design principles and techniques, you can improve your
ability, increase your confidence and begin to create pieces
which reflect your own style.

# Principles of design

No one can be taught design as such; however, what you can learn is how to look at the world around you, adapt what you see and change it into a design that is new, exciting and uniquely your own.

There is no better way to start thinking about design than to look at as much jewellery as you possibly can. Visit museums and study jewellery from every age and culture. Look in jeweller's windows and go to markets and junk shops. Buy old bits of jewellery and take them to pieces, so that you can see exactly how they were put together. Gradually you will begin to get an idea of the kind of jewellery that interests you and of the design directions you want to pursue.

Inspiration can come from any source, so do not confine yourself to just looking at jewellery. When visiting a museum you may find exciting shapes and patterns in wrought iron, textiles, carpets, sculpture, decorative door handles, keys, friezes, weapons, royal regalia, canoe decorations or mayoral chains of office. Design ideas can be inspired by almost anything – from electrical components to plants, fish, shells, insects and seaweed. Most professional designers are compulsive collectors of magazines, books, postcards, and interesting objects from shells to handbag catches. Everything you look at could be a possible basis for a piece of jewellery, so design is really a process of rejection and selection as well as inspiration.

Inspiration has to be translated from object to design. The best way of developing your ideas is to make sketches. When I visited the Alhambra in Spain, I was immediately inspired by its formal patterns and subtle colours. I spent three days sketching it – first overall and then picking out specific shapes and patterns. If you do not have the time to make detailed sketches you can take photographs. Always travel with a pocket notebook, as you may suddenly see something which inspires you – the necklace of a woman sitting opposite you on a bus, or the design of the stained glass in a church window, also it will be of benefit to you to practise drawing life studies – of apples say – to develop a feeling for conveying three dimensions. The more experience you have in drawing such objects, the easier you will find it to translate the ideas in your mind to designs on paper.

**Necklace and pendants by Castellani - 1865**
This ornate and delicate design is a replica of a classical Greek diadem. Made in pure gold, it is a fine example of chasing, repoussé, filigree and granulation work. If you see jewellery like this in a museum and feel inspired to make a similar piece, you might think in terms of casting or stamping units, or else you could pick out part of the design and adapt it.

## Choosing your materials and techniques

Once you reach the stage where you are ready to translate your ideas into reality, it is time to think about what materials you could use and indeed whether your design is technically possible to make. In the early stages, you will find it easier to start with brooches, earrings and pendants. Necklaces and bracelets are more demanding in terms of both design and technical skill, while it is particularly advisable to gain some experience before you attempt to design a ring. This is because the restrictions imposed by the form make it very difficult to be original.

Let us suppose you have seen a frieze that has inspired you with its shapes, patterns and colours. You have sketched or photographed it and it has given you an idea for a bangle. The next stage might be to make a cardboard model with the pattern drawn on to it; you could also use plasticine, metal foil or self-hardening clay. Such models will help you to see how the piece could best be made and what materials you could use. You will then have to decide whether your design would look most effective stamped, engraved, inlaid or pierced into the metal; whether you will want to plate or colour it, and whether you will be decorating it with stones or granulation. When you have decided on all of these points, you might want to use another part of the frieze as design inspiration for a pair of matching earrings. The most important thing is to know in your mind what you want the finished piece to be and how you want it to look.

Once you have found an idea that appeals to you, before you begin work you must make sure that it fulfills all the practical functions of a piece of jewellery – after all, jewellery is designed to be worn, as well as looking attractive.

## Wearing jewellery

Most people know what suits them best and what they feel comfortable wearing. However, I feel that it is worth considering how to wear jewellery, as sometimes people pay less attention to their choice of jewellery than they do to the rest of their wardrobe. It is a pity to see lovely pieces of jewellery worn with uncomplementary clothing or combined with other pieces which are badly matched. Your clothing should show off your jewellery and your jewellery should enhance your clothing and your appearance.

Before buying or wearing a piece of jewellery you should first assess your physical build. Your choice of

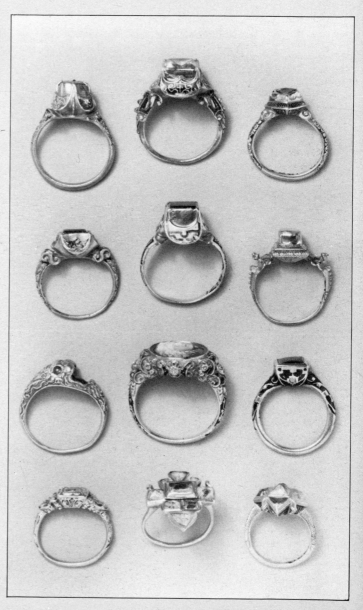

**Sixteenth century rings**
For centuries rings have been considered the most significant item of jewellery. Despite the restrictions of its circular form, the approach to ring design has been amazingly varied. These 16th century gold rings incorporate unusual settings, delicate enamel work and fine engraving.

earrings, for example, should take into account the shape of your face and the length of your neck. If you have a round face you may look better with long, dangling earrings than with circular clip-on ones; whereas dangling earrings may be inappropriate if you have a short neck or a long face. It is important to think of earrings and necklaces as a frame for your face. Unexpected combinations can work, but they must be worn with confidence.

Earrings, bracelets and necklaces are usually chosen to complement each other and to enhance an outfit, whereas rings are both more separate and more personal. Rings are the only items of jewellery you yourself can constantly see and enjoy so, while they should harmonize with the other pieces you are wearing, they can be more individual. However, you must consider the shape of your hands and fingers. Chunky rings do not suit chubby, short fingers and small delicate rings will look absurd if you have large, practical hands with broad fingers.

Your colouring might also have an influence on your choice of jewellery. If you have blue eyes you might choose to wear sapphires rather than emeralds, for example. A pale complexion and very blond hair will be enhanced by wearing silver rather than gold; whereas gold will look particularly spectacular against a dark skin.

Having assessed yourself, the next step is to examine your wardrobe - the clothes you wear and what they say about your personality. If you like frilly, feminine clothes in soft pastels your jewellery should be chosen to enhance this image; it might include delicate filigree, pale stones like citrine, aquamarine or rose quartz and pearls. If you have a flamboyant personality and enjoy wearing strong colours, large, bold pieces of jewellery will probably suit you the best.

Once you have considered your physical appearance and your wardrobe, there are also some general rules about wearing jewellery which you should bear in mind. On the whole, it is unwise to wear too much jewellery, since, unless the pieces are very carefully chosen, one may well clash with another.

Be very careful about mixing different types of metal, or a variety of colours. When you are deciding what to wear, think of a parallel, like decorating a room and choosing colours for curtains and carpets. An unusual mix can be very striking, but it is more likely to be disastrous unless you are very confident about your taste. If, for example, your overall colour scheme is white and lilac, your outfit will probably not be enhanced by a ruby ring. Gold and silver can be mixed successfully if there is enough of each to balance, but one silver ring may look out of place against a mass of gold and vice versa.

If you mix fine gold rings set with precious stones with a costume jewellery bracelet in cheap gold, the latter will downgrade the rings, whereas the bracelet worn on its own might be very effective. If your clothing itself is decorated with appliqué or fancy buttons, you should wear very simple jewellery, as ornate earrings and brooches will detract from the impression you are seeking to give with your dress.

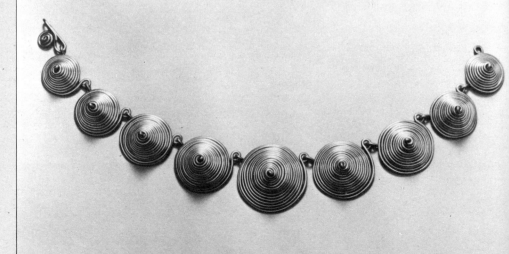

**Necklace by Alexander Calder**
Jewellery is inextricably linked with other art forms and many great artists such as Salvador Dali or Pablo Picasso have used jewellery as a medium of expression. This necklace in forged, beaten wire coils is clearly related to Calder's mobiles and sculpture.

Though many people think style is something innate, it can also be developed. By observing a few basic rules you can make sure that the jewellery you wear enhances your physical appearance and adds that special finishing touch to whatever you are wearing.

### Choosing colours and shapes

Colour plays an important part in jewellery design. Some materials seem to complement each other, while others clash. Ivory, for example, looks better set in silver rather than gold. The coolness of the silver emphasizes the colour of the ivory whereas gold tends to dominate it. Lapis lazuli, on the other hand, can be set in gold or silver, while rubies and garnets look better in gold. Be very careful about mixing stones of different colours. If you are unsure about which colours look well together you should look at jewellery in museums, or at the work of professional designers to see whether the colours you have in mind can be combined successfully. Remember, however, that some museum pieces have mellowed over the years, so the original colours of metals and stones may have softened. A modern replica might look brash or garish – particularly if you cannot afford materials of the same quality as those used in the original.

Shape is another important consideration when you are thinking about your design. A necklace that is wide or heavy at shoulder level and then tapers will not only look out of proportion but will not fit properly. The weight of a necklace should always be at its lowest point. Clip earrings which are too large will slip off the earlobes. Drop earrings comprising a small shape suspended between two larger shapes may look rather awkward and unrelated.

### Light

If you are working with translucent stones, such as quartz or moonstones you will ruin their delicate effect by combining them with strongly-coloured stones or heavy metals. Translucent drop earrings must be hung with great care for maximum effect. The system used to hang the drop should be as light as possible, involving the minimum use of metal. A small bead of the same stone as the drop or a complementary stone may be most effective.

Dangling earrings in glass and perspex are particularly attractive, as striking light effects can be achieved with faceting and by using an unobtrusive setting. Settings are equally important when you are hanging precious stones in drop earrings. The light should be allowed to shine through the stones, thus enhancing their natural colour. The cut, or faceting, of precious stones produces different light effects. A brilliant cut gives the most sparkle, but the effect may

be dazzling if the stone is large. If you have a really beautiful stone the setting should be designed to show it off; it should not take attention away from the stone.

### Weight and proportion

Jewellery must be comfortable to wear. If it is heavy or bulky, it may not simply look clumsy – it will be an actual physical burden. If you are designing a large pair of earrings in metal, a solid shape will probably be too heavy to hang from the ear, whereas a hollow construction will make the earrings practical. If a brooch is too heavy it may tear the material to which it is pinned, particularly delicate satin or silks.

Proportion is particularly important when you are designing earrings. The back of a hanging earring is as important as the front so the design must be pictured from all sides and angles. The method of hanging must be carefully considered too, since the balance of the hanging shape will effect the earrings' proportions.

### Techniques

Once you have decided on your design, and thought about colour, weight, balance and proportion, it is time to think about the more practical question of the techniques you might use.

If your shape is solid or sculptural, it may be best to carve it in wax, take it to the platers and have it cast in metal. A very delicate design might be executed in fine silver wire which can be twisted and bent, or else in fine openwork. If your ideas are based around surface pattern, you will have to consider textures and decide which techniques you can use to achieve the effect you have in mind. If your design requires colour, you will be thinking in terms of stones that will complement each other or of metals which can be mixed or coloured. Designing jewellery is both fun and rewarding. As with any form of design, it is advisable to start off by learning the basic theoretical and practical principles before you try something too ambitious. Not every idea will result in a successful piece, but do not give up too quickly. If you have thought of an idea and made a piece which does not wholly satisfy you, then make it again - and again. By the fourth attempt you may be getting near to the ideal in your mind, and along the way, you will have learnt a great deal about construction and technique. Never throw an idea out until you have exploited it to the full.

Once you have explored the different techniques of jewellery making and experimented with designing a variety of pieces, you will find that some appeal to you more than others. Gradually you will develop an individual style, while the more experienced you become, the easier you will find it to make attractive and original pieces of jewellery.

**Damascus earrings by Dinny Hall**
The shapes of these tiered chandelier earrings are drawn from the formal patterns in Moorish and Spanish tiles and friezes. I made numerous sketches until I was satisfied that the shapes, when strung together, would complement each other and form an attractive frame for the face. The light openwork design of the earrings is decorative, and makes them comfortable to wear. The earrings have been decorated with granulation and the silver oxidized to create a subtle shimmer of colour as they move.

**Brooch and earrings by Dinny Hall**
When I visited the cathedral of Notre-Dame in Paris I felt so inspired by one of the magnificent rose windows that I painstakingly drew each detail of it. Later I designed a brooch which echoes the actual design of the window. The finished brooch is openwork brass, silver plated and oxidized, with decorative granulation and ornately-set, cabochon amethyst quartz. I set brightly-coloured butterfly wings beneath the quartz, so that they glow through the translucent lilac of the stones.
The earrings are based on formal Islamic designs. In the centre of each earring I have hung a costume pearl, dyed gun-metal purple to complement the colours of the oxidized metal.

**Button earrings by Madelaine Cole**
These button earrings in dyed and etched aluminium reflect Madelaine Cole's fascination with Islamic design and calligraphy. Her ideas are gathered from museums, books, postcards and private collections of Islamic art.

**Necklace by Charmian Inman**
The inspiration for this chunky necklace comes from African beads and textiles. The bold pattern has been oxidized on to the silver units and then lacquered. The lacquer fixes the design and gives the metal a lovely matt finish. The structure of the necklace is as unusual as its appearance. The silver tubing is filled with cork and the units are strung together with plaited black silk thread. This system joins the units tightly together, while allowing flexibility. The necklace is then tied around the neck.

**Mask brooches by Tom Binns** These three brooches were the precursers of a commercial range of jewellery, using masks in many different materials and sizes. Tom Binns' designs are a personal expression of his feelings, although he thinks that the design of these brooches may have been influenced subconsciously by Viennese masks.

Ceramic mask with brittle matt finish *(left)*; 'The deaf leading the blind' in ebony and ivory *(centre)*; porcelain mask, fired black and set in silver *(right)*.

**Serpent brooch by Hilary Beane**
This piece is part of a collection of stage jewellery made for Liza Minelli. It is a striking combination of tiny beads, rhinestones and gold fleur-de-lis.

**'Crown and executioner's axe' by Hilary Beane**
Hilary Beane is fascinated by royal regalia and created this colourful piece to symbolize the power of royalty through the ages. She has used a multitude of tiny beads and stones, mixed with metal stampings and pearls set into papier mâché. The crown and brooch have individual pins - an idea based on Celtic cloak brooches.

## Alhambra Collection by Dinny Hall

I first saw the Alhambra Palace *(below)* several years ago on a visit to Grenada, and immediately felt inspired by its architectural form and the rich subtlety of its colours. The beautiful shades of gold, turquoise and purple, mingling with the mass of formal pattern and the fountains of cascading water, were to suggest the idea for a jewellery collection.

I made many sketches of the palace and later studied books on it. I isolated patterns and experimented with them until I found the most suitable ones for jewellery. I then made metal models for each design to test the balance.

### Reflections of colour

The shimmering shades of gold, purple and blue found in the Alhambra are recaptured in the subtle gradations of colour in these earrings. Their shape is also drawn directly from the intricate patterns used everywhere in the stonework and tiles of the palace.

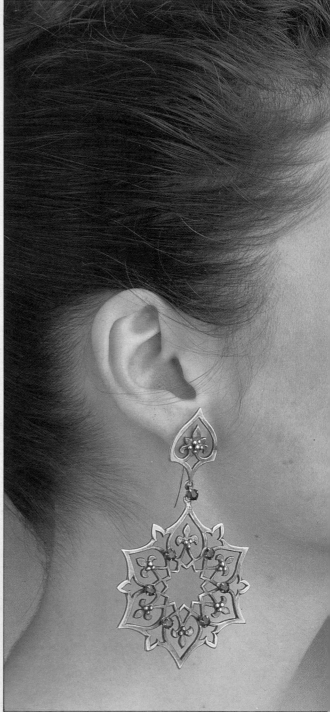

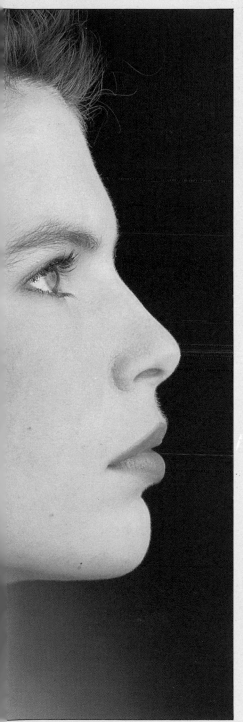

**Precious stones**
The plain antiqued silver of this ring and bracelet provide the perfect setting for exotic, vividly-coloured stones.

**A wealth of patterns**
In my designs I aimed to recapture the formal intricacy of the Alhambra, where the qualities of delicacy and strength are perfectly combined.

**Jane Adam**
Jane Adam is interested primarily in colour and pattern; the shape comes later. Her colours, particularly in the pieces illustrated, are influenced by photographs of tropical fish and by the soft shades of porcelain. She feels that the metallic lustres of ceramics are closely related to the anodic film on aluminium. The pattern of her pieces is drawn largely from Japanese textiles, which are made up of many layers of woven fabric. She achieves a textural effect by imposing one colourful pattern over a complementary pattern of shapes or curving lines which has been etched into the aluminium. While the patterns that she uses are derived from a combination of design sources, the carving of her shapes is the most individual aspect of her work.

**Earringbrooches by Jane Adam**
The three pieces shown here can be worn as brooches, with the wire fastening threaded through the material, or as earrings. Each has been carved in aluminium, etched, anodized and then painted with dyes to obtain a delicate pattern which is both textural and colourful.

### Tom McEwan

Tom McEwan works mostly in titanium and regards colour as the most important aspect of his jewellery. His bold shapes are spontaneous, inspired by the swooping lines of fashion drawings. He executes rough sketches of his patterns on paper and then meticulously marks them on to the titanium. Colour is applied electrolytically in layers, fine gradations being added with an electro-conductive paintbrush.

### Bangles and hairpin by Tom McEwan

The lovely patterns and colours of these pieces are typical of Tom's work.

### Annabelle Ely

Annabelle Ely sells her jewellery to Liberty of London, among others, and her work is also displayed in galleries around the United Kingdom.

### Earrings and bracelet by Annabelle Ely

These striking earrings were pictured on the cover of *Vogue* and are available in many different colours. They are made from discs of tapering silver, edged with silver wire. A bright hand-threaded silk tassel is strung through the centre of each earring. The matching bangle echoes the earrings' bold simplicity.

**Comb and earrings by Madelaine Cole**
The inspiration for this black, anodized aluminium hair comb is drawn from Japanese designs. The comb is pierced out and then etched with lace patterns, creating a textural effect.
The matching button earrings, in the same basic shape as her Islamic earrings, show how a simple shape can be transformed by using different surface patterns.

**Madelaine Cole**
Madelaine Cole sells her work to Harvey Nichols and Liberty of London and to stores in New York, Japan and Australia. Her favourite material is aluminium which she etches and dyes. She likes classic colours - black, red, silver, gold - and strong, simple shapes. She derives her ideas from many sources, including museums, books and postcards. Victoriana, particularly lace, furniture fittings, mirrors and textiles, provides inspiration for her patterns and textures, while her shapes are often influenced by African and Japanese artefacts.

**Hair combs by Madelaine Cole**
The delicate, tactile patterns on these combs have been etched into the aluminium.

**Fred Riche**

Fred Riche works mainly to commission, often taking up to three or four weeks to perfect an individual piece. He draws his inspiration from intangible sources, such as the breaking of ocean waves or the wind rushing through leaves and grass. Sometimes he becomes obsessed by a particular feeling, or mood, and he will design and make several pieces of work until he has achieved a visual expression that satisfies him. His expertise in the application and colouring of enamel enables him to experiment with technique and design, achieving effects which are strikingly individual in form and tone.

**Standing brooch by Fred Riche**

The swirling colours and scalloped shape of this brooch echo the power and grace of breaking waves. Made from repousséd silver, tiny gold wires and subtle shades of enamel, it can be worn as a brooch or displayed as an ornament.

**Necklace by Fred Riche**

Enamelled shapes, pearls and gold make an eye-catching combination. The box catch is cleverly incorporated into the design, forming a spherical shape when fastened.

**Martin Baker**
Martin Baker's clients have included royalty, the aristocracy, Arab princes and well-known art collectors. His pieces are exhibited in the Victoria and Albert museum, London. His source of inspiration comes from a combination of natural forms and Art Nouveau. He is fascinated by the patterns formed on glass by frost or condensation and by the delicate anatomy of insects. He collects books and photographs and then spends time drawing before he begins his three-dimensional designs.

**Snail box by Martin Baker**
Humour and fine workmanship combine to create a unique piece in silver and horn.

**Earrings by Martin Baker**
Martin's jewellery is delicate and very simple. These 18 carat gold and frosted glass earrings are typical of his style.

### Hilary Beane

Hilary Beane sells her work to stores throughout America and her private clients include Liza Minelli and Madonna. She is an eclectic designer, influenced by 'almost anything that happened in ornamentation before the 12th and 13th century'. She works by isolating shapes from Celtic, Roman, Islamic, Byzantine and Etruscan art and combining them in unusual ways, using untraditional techniques.

### Necklace by Hilary Beane

A baroque, fantasy necklace created from pearls, stamped, gold plated leaves and flowers, turquoise tubing set with crystals, gold-coloured metal and rhinestones.

### Brooch by Hilary Beane

This colourful design is made from papier mâché, set with dozens of gold-coloured beads, rhinestones and crystal.

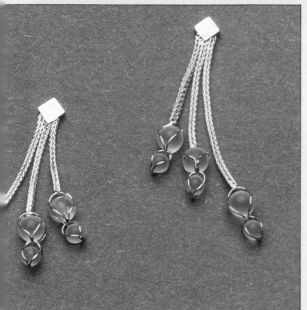

### Andrew Logan

Andrew Logan is probably best known for his remarkable sculptures which are made up from many pieces of coloured broken mirror and glass and have been exhibited around the world. His jewellery is an extension of his sculpture and has been featured in advertising, fashion magazines, films and videos. He finds he is unable to derive ideas purely from books or museums, so his inspiration springs from trips to countries such as Turkey, India and Egypt.

### Necklace and earrings by Andrew Logan

This sumptuous necklace was inspired by a visit to Egypt and is a form of homage to the Pharaohs. Made from epoxy modelling clay, the necklace is moulded into the shape of a torso and embedded with hundreds of tiny pearls, pieces of broken glass and coloured rhinestones. The matching pyramid earrings are made from broken mirror and gold glitter.

### Earrings, bangles and ring by Andrew Logan

The bangles and ring have bought metal bases which have been covered with epoxy clay embedded with glass and stones. The earrings are made from broken Christmas tree baubles and glitter.

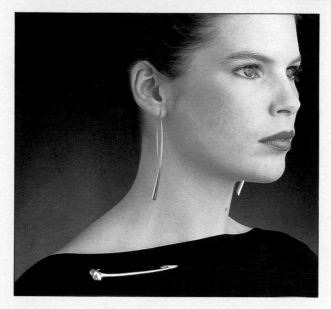

**Earrings and brooch by Tom Binns**
Carved from silver, then gold plated, these pieces bring to mind the words of the sculptor Brancussi, 'simplicity is complexity'.

**Tom Binns**
Tom Binns makes use of the technical aspects of his design training, but he feels that it is his rejection of the principles of formal jewellery design which has lead to the development of his peculiarly individual style. He sells his jewellery all over the world - Germany, Italy, France, America and Australia and his work has been worn by David Bowie, Elton John and Michael Jackson. He is currently moving away from fashion towards jewellery as pure art to be hung on walls or displayed in galleries.

**Madame Butterfly by Tom Binns**
A clever combination of objets trouvés form a brooch which is as attractive as it is unusual.

**Food for thought by Tom Binns**
Elegant, yet humorous, these earrings and matching brooch show that, with imagination, everyday objects can be transformed into stunning jewellery.

**Cartier jewellery**
The great commercial jewel houses, such as Cartier in Paris, are a complete contrast to the small workshop with its highly individual designs. Cartier, founded in 1847 by Louis Francois Cartier, is renowned for its classic jewellery that mirrors the fashion of its own time and yet is ageless.

**Bracelets - 1940s**
These three bracelets are typical of Cartier's 1940s style. Note the way each catch is perfectly integrated into the overall pattern, creating a very simple but effective design.

**Brooch - 1950s**
A simple setting in red and gold displays this magnificent smoky quartz to its full advantage.

**Brooches - 1940s**
The design of these brooches
is extremely simple but their
use of precious materials is
striking – a plain buckle
shape in carved rock crystal,
tiny sapphires and tinted
chalcedony *(top)*; a figure of
eight in white gold,
diamonds and pearls
*(bottom)*.

**David Webb ring - 1960s**
Although this is a large ring,
the translucence of the
crystal and the delicacy of the
design gives an impression of
lightness.

# Stones and cuts/1

Gemmology is a specialist subject in its own right and lies beyond the scope of this book. However, it is important to know some of the basic facts about gemstones when selecting stones for jewellery making.

Stones are divided popularly into two groups – precious and semi-precious. Diamonds, emeralds, rubies and sapphires are generally considered to be precious stones; while semi-precious stones cover a vast range from aquamarine to rose quartz. This division is not a particularly useful one, especially in terms of price, as a fine opal or pearl can be more valuable than some precious stones. It is preferable, therefore, to use the name gemstone as a generic description of the whole range of stones.

**Types of stone**
The most valuable stone in the beryl group is emerald. The best quality stones are a rich, pure green, but they also come in a variety of shades. Emerald is a comparatively soft stone which affects the way it is cut – usually cabochon or step-cut. The other important stone in this group is aquamarine. It is a pale blue in colour and, although less valuable than emerald, top

quality stones are much sought after.

Rubies and sapphires are both members of the corundrum group. Although rubies are harder than emeralds, they are brittle and are generally step-cut. Sapphires range in colour from a rich blue through white, green and yellow so, when buying one, it is important to specify the colour you require. Sapphires are cut in the same way as rubies.

Diamond is the hardest natural material known, which is why jewellers have taken centuries to perfect techniques for polishing and faceting these beautiful stones. Diamonds range in colour from a brilliant white through to yellow, blue, brown and pink.

There are so many semi-precious stones that it is impossible to mention all of them. I have selected what I consider to be some of the most interesting and colourful of the stones available.

The largest group of semi-precious stones are the quartzes. They vary in colour and can be opaque, translucent or clear. They include amethyst, citrine, rose quartz, smoky quartz, chalcedony, chrysoprase, jasper, agate, onyx and cornelian. One of the most beautiful stones of the quartz group is topaz which,

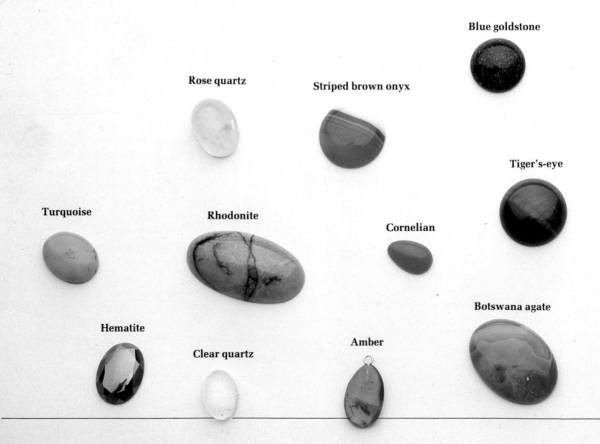

Blue goldstone

Rose quartz

Striped brown onyx

Tiger's-eye

Turquoise

Rhodonite

Cornelian

Botswana agate

Hematite

Clear quartz

Amber

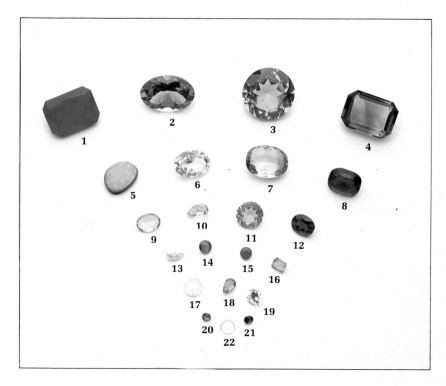

1 synthetic ruby; 2 smoky quartz; 3 synthetic amethyst; 4 smoky quartz; 5 opal; 6 citrine; 7 citrine; 8 amethyst; 9 peridot; 10 aquamarine; 11 topaz; 12 garnet; 13 natural baroque pearl; 14 sapphire; 15 ruby; 16 emerald; 17 jelly opal; 18 rose quartz; 19 diamond; 20 emerald; 21 tourmaline; 22 moonstone.

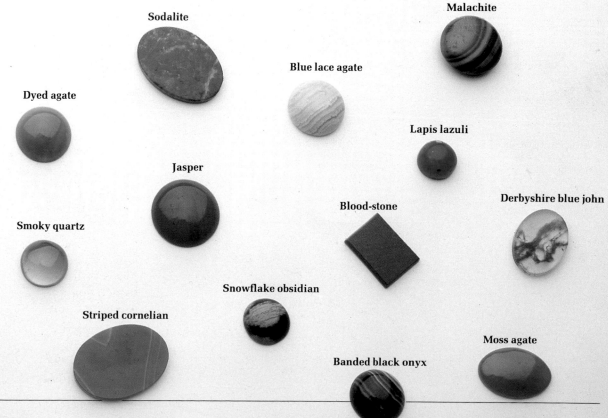

Sodalite

Malachite

Blue lace agate

Dyed agate

Lapis lazuli

Jasper

Derbyshire blue john

Blood-stone

Smoky quartz

Snowflake obsidian

Striped cornelian

Moss agate

Banded black onyx

# Stones and cuts/2

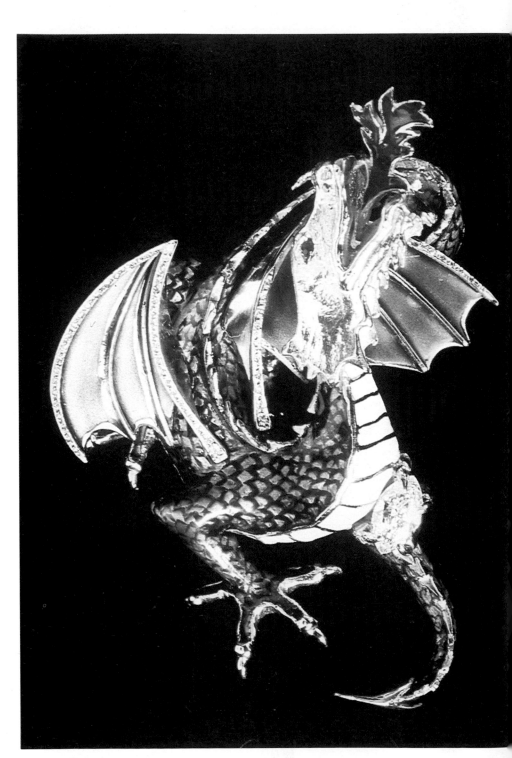

**Dragon brooch by
Martin Baker**
This elaborate gold and
enamel brooch, set with
rubies and diamonds, has an
interesting history. It was
commissioned as the prize
for a treasure hunt and was
hidden in a castle in Wales –
hence the dragon design, as
the dragon is Wales' national
emblem. The marquise cut
diamond is set into the
dragon's claws, almost as
though it were the prize
itself. This arrangement
fulfills the basic purposes of
any setting; it is not only
extremely original, but also
displays the stone to
maximum advantage.

although generally thought of as being a warm sherry colour, ranges from colourless to blue-green.

One of the strangest and most beautiful of all gemstones is the opal, with its brilliant flashes of colour. It is a delicate and unstable stone, easily chipped or cracked and damaged by heat or grease. Turquoise and lapis lazuli have both been used in jewellery making for centuries. Good turquoise should be a vivid blue but, unless treated with care, it can be reduced to a dull green by contact with water or grease. Lapis lazuli should be a deep aquamarine with gold flecks. It is ideal for inlay because of its softness.

Garnet is the collective name for a variety of silicate materials ranging from blood red to purple, green, orange, black and yellow. They are a popular jeweller's stone, particularly when 'ruby' coloured.

There are even more varieties of feldspar than there are of quartz, but very few of them are gemstones. The best known are the lovely milky-white moonstone, and amazonite which, when polished, is a rich green.

Jade is a general term which descibes jadite and nephrite. Jadite is the most valuable of the two and comes in a variety of colours from emerald green to brown, red and white. It is an ideal material for carving, being both soft and firm.

## Gems of organic origin

Most gemstones are minerals but there are some, such as pearls, jet, coral and amber, which are products of the animal and vegetable world. Real pearls are produced by oysters and mussels, without any human intervention, and are the most valuable. Cultured pearls are formed by inserting a foreign object into the mollusc shell. Natural pearls can be perfectly round or they can be shaped – pear, seed, freshwater and baroque. They also vary in colour from pinky-white to black, blue, yellow and green.

Coral is the skeleton of a warm-water marine animal. Gem coral is mostly pinks and red-oranges, but there is also the rarer black and brown coral. Jet, which was very popular in Victorian times for mourning jewellery, is a fossil wood which can be cut and polished like a mineral. It is brittle, but easy to carve. Amber is the fossilized resin of an extinct pine tree. It comes in a variety of colours from red through to yellow, ochre and orange. The most expensive is the clear, orange amber. The softness of amber makes it easy to cut and polish.

## Synthetic stones

There are many artificial stones on the market. Some of these are so realistic that only a trained jeweller's eye can detect the difference. The artificial diamond, known as cubic zirconia, is the most effective of the fake stones. Turquoise can be sold in a compressed form – crushed and reconstituted – which enhances its colour, but reduces its value.

## Cutting and faceting

Most of the stones used in jewellery making are cut. The simplest cut is the cabochon. It is a smooth dome-shaped cut with no facets and can be oval, circular, square or elliptical. The base is almost always flat, but it can also be concave to give more colour to the stone. Facets are cut on a gemstone so that the flat planes will exploit the refraction and reflection of light, giving the stone brilliance and colour. Faceting is a highly skilled technique which no amateur jeweller should attempt.

The character of the stone will determine the nature of its setting. Cabochon cuts are easier to set and allow greater scope for originality. The setting of a faceted stone, however, tends to be more formal and to require greater expertise. The aim is usually to display the stone to its maximum advantage. On the whole, it is preferable to have faceted stones set professionally, particularly if the stone is valuable.

## Choosing stones

It is advisable to read some specialist gem books before you begin buying stones, as it is important to know what qualities you should look for. When you visit a gem dealer you will be faced with a bewildering array of stones, each varying in quality and price. Your choice will be governed largely by the price, but there are other factors which you should take into consideration.

It is essential to choose a reputable dealer as, to a great extent, you will have to trust his advice. This means it is very unwise to buy stones from bazaars or other exotic outlets when you travel, as you are apt to be cheated unless you are very experienced in choosing stones. It is also not worth buying uncut stones, since lapidary work is very expensive.

The most important characteristics of stones are hardness and colour. Hardness is an important consideration when choosing stones for a specific piece of jewellery, as a relatively soft stone may become scratched or chipped if set in a ring or a bracelet, and is probably more suited to a necklace or a brooch. If a stone is best known for its colour - lapis lazuli, turquoise, citrine, amethyst, jade and garnet for instance - the richer and truer the colour, the better the stone. This difference should be reflected in its price.

Check the clarity of stones by holding them up to the light. Watch out for flaws and chips and make sure that the stones are priced accordingly. Always examine the quality of the cutting. The curve of a cabochon should be true and the bottom should be flat or it will be difficult to set. The facets of a stone should be balanced and evenly cut.

# Elementary jewellery

While I do not believe that people need formal design training in order to make attractive, functional jewellery, it is important to have some knowledge of the basic materials, tools and techniques the professionals use to create their own jewellery to the best possible standard.

You should start by learning as much as possible about the properties of your materials – particularly metal which is the basis of most jewellery making. However, you do not have to master any complicated theories or technical data – the practical aspects are far more important at this stage. I have tried to make this section as direct and simple as possible, by combining an introduction to the basic techniques with practical step-by-step projects. In this way, after some initial experiment, you will be able to put what you have learnt into practice by creating pieces of jewellery that are attractive in themselves. You will probably find that you master some techniques more quickly than others. However, you should explore the possibilities of each technique to the full, since you may well find that you produce your best work using a technique that you discarded initially. You will be able to buy most of the tools and equipment you need at your local hardware store, since many of the pliers and hand tools are non-specialized. Hardware stores are also a good source of supply for some of the chemicals you need, plus epoxy glues, brass chain and rings, brushes, containers, turpentine and cleaning fluids. More specialized items of equipment can be bought at craft stores and jeweller's supply stores.

# Setting up your own workshop

You do not need a large amount of space to set up a jewellery workshop. It is possible to convert almost any area – attic, scullery, cellar, shed or garage – into a perfectly functional work place. However, it is neither practical nor safe to use part of your kitchen or any main living area; making jewellery can be messy and you will be using potentially dangerous chemicals.

## Ventilation and light

Ventilation and light are the most important factors to be taken into consideration when setting up a workshop. You must have adequate ventilation – either large windows or an extractor fan – for times when you use chemicals. It is always preferable to work in natural light, but if you do have to rely on artificial light, make sure it is bright and conveniently positioned.

## Water and electricity

It is preferable to have running water in the workshop, but if this is not possible, there should be a source of supply reasonably close to hand. An electricity supply is vital both for lighting and for equipment. Keep the position of power points in mind when you plan the layout of your workshop.

## Space

Your workshop must be large enough to accommodate a workbench; shelves, cupboards and drawers for storing tools, chemicals and materials and a surface area for drills and polishers. Ideally you should also allow some space for reference materials.

## Furniture

The most important item of workshop furniture is a jeweller's workbench. This should be about 90cm high and built of solid wood, with a semicircular piece cut out of the top to enable you to get close to your work. It is preferable to buy a ready-made workbench, rather than to attempt to make your own. You will also need an adjustable swivel chair, or stool; a solid surface for hammering, such as a sturdy table or a section of tree trunk, a refrigerator for chemicals and acrylic resins and hooks for hanging up tools, coils of wire etc.

## Tools

It is not necessary to start with all the tools mentioned in this book, but the following are essential if you want to make professional-looking jewellery: jeweller's saw, pliers, files, tweezers, shears, drill, soldering block, filing peg, pickling chemicals, blow torch or butane torch, flux, hammers, mallet, snips, steel ruler, emery paper and sticks, wheel with rouge and tripoli mops, ring triblet, scriber, cleansing brushes, wire brush and steel block.

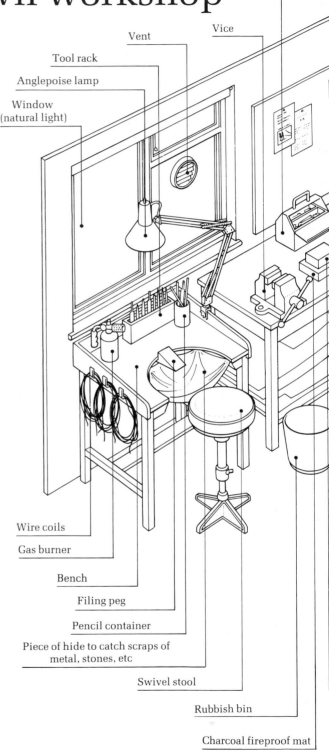

Toolbox

Vice

Vent

Tool rack

Anglepoise lamp

Window (natural light)

Wire coils

Gas burner

Bench

Filing peg

Pencil container

Piece of hide to catch scraps of metal, stones, etc

Swivel stool

Rubbish bin

Charcoal fireproof mat

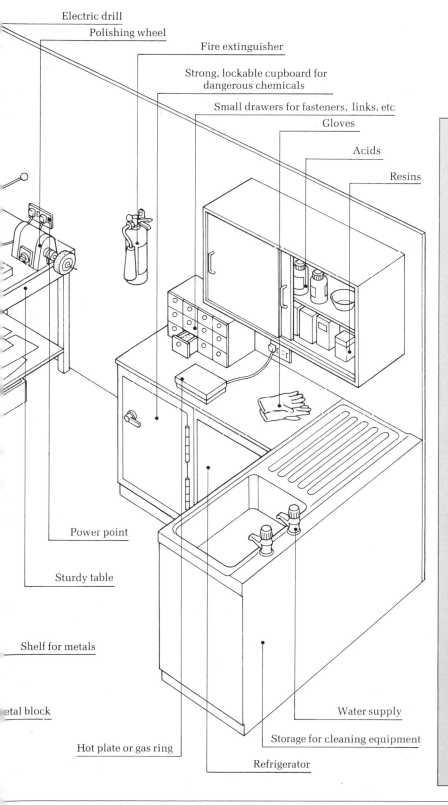

Electric drill

Polishing wheel

Fire extinguisher

Strong, lockable cupboard for dangerous chemicals

Small drawers for fasteners, links, etc

Gloves

Acids

Resins

Power point

Sturdy table

Shelf for metals

etal block

Hot plate or gas ring

Refrigerator

Storage for cleaning equipment

Water supply

## HEALTH AND SAFETY

A jewellery workshop is probably no more dangerous than the average kitchen, but it is important to be aware of potential hazards. Most precautions are common sense, but there are some areas which need special attention, particularly if you have young children.

### Chemicals
1. Containers should be securely fastened and stored well out of the reach of children.
2. When you are working with chemicals, or any other harmful substance, always wear rubber gloves without holes.
3. Keep food and drink well away from all acids, fluxes, lead, resins and polishes.
4. Always work near a supply of running water, particularly when you are using acids.

### Equipment
1. Do not allow young children into your workshop unaccompanied.
2. Tie back long hair when using polishers and drills.
3. It is advisable not to wear dangling jewellery or clothing with flapping sleeves.
4. It is sensible to wear closed shoes, in case you drop a piece of redhot metal or some heavy item of equipment.

### General safety
1. Turn off all gas appliances as soon as you have finished using them.
2. Keep a fire extinguisher and a first aid box in your workshop. The first aid box should contain plaster, antiseptic and a salve for minor burns.
3. Wear protective goggles when necessary.
4. Do not work under inadequate light, or use a chair which is the wrong height.

# Tools and accessories

When you begin making jewellery, you only need a few pieces of equipment. Other items can be bought as you need them. The tools illustrated will cover all your initial requirements. **1** curved snips or shears; **2** straight snips; **3** parallel pliers; **4** curved burnisher;

**5** scissors; **6** wooden mallet – or a rubber, leather or plastic-covered lead mallet; **7** scalpel; **8** ball pein hammer; **9** riveting hammer; **10** steel rulers; **11** sheets of emery paper, ranging from fine grain to coarse grain; **12** emery stick.

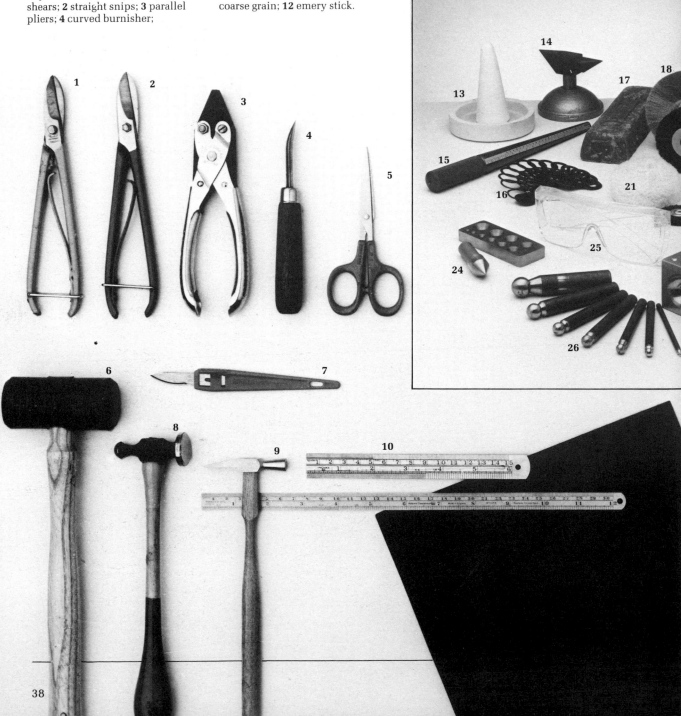

**13** borax cone and tray – other fluxes are available for different solders; **14** bick iron for making cones and acute curves; **15** standard ring stake or triblet; **16** set of ring sizes; **17** tripoli – in varying grades of abrasion; **18** brass wire wheel; **19** hard felt mop; **20** buffing brush; **21** rouge mop; **22** small buffing brush; **23** butane gas torch; **24** collet plate and punch; **25** goggles **26** set of doming punches; **27** doming block.

**28** wire cutters; **29** narrow-tipped pliers; **30** round-nosed pliers; **31** all-purpose pliers; **32** half-round pliers; **33** spring tweezers for clamping metal during soldering; **34** brass tweezers; **35** plastic tweezers for chemicals and acids; **36** scriber; **37** round needle file; **38** half-round needle file; **39** flat needle file; **40** square file; **41** all-purpose file; **42** half-round file; **43** steel block; **44** centre punch; **45** dividers; **46** jeweller's saw and a selection of blades ranging from coarse to fine.

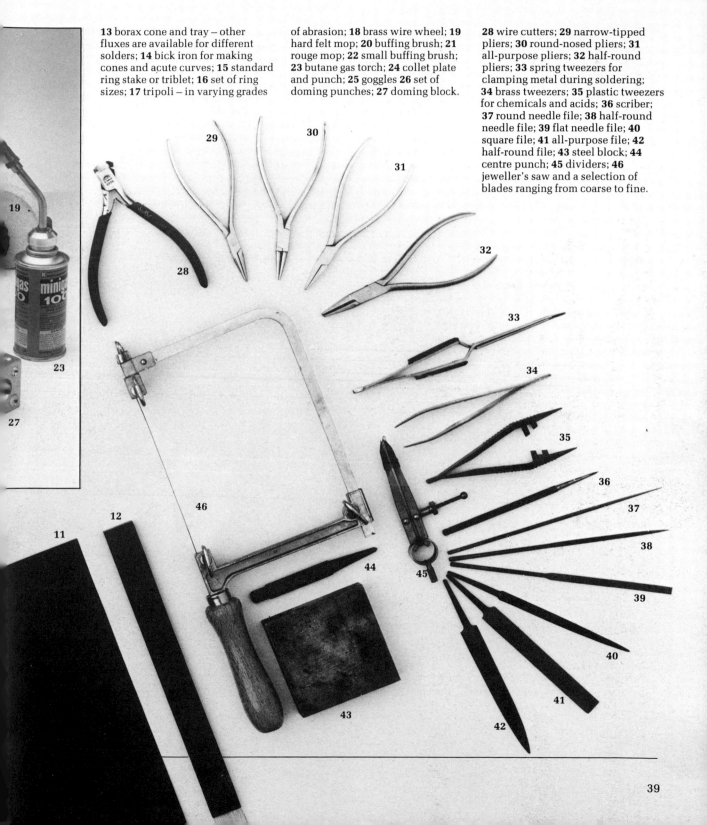

# Jewellery basics/1

Soldering, drilling, engraving and embossing are all skills which we tend to associate with contemporary jewellery making, rather than with the jewellery of the past. Today, the choice is so wide that modern jewellers are able to choose exactly the ones to suit a particular creation.

**Non-ferrous metals**
The term 'non-ferrous' means that the metals it describes do not contain iron. Precious metals all fall into this category.

Gold is the most commonly used of the precious metals. The standard by which you judge its quality is defined as so many carats, which indicates its quality. Do not confuse the term's use in this context with its use when applied to precious stones; in the latter case it is used as a a measure of weight.

**24 carat gold** is known as fine gold. It is completely pure and so is very soft and yellow in colour. This softness means that it is not used in the construction of jewellery; it is mainly used in gold plating.

**22 carat gold** is yellow or light yellow. It is not pure metal, but an alloy of gold and fine silver or copper. You will find that the percentages of pure metal to alloy are specified in parts per thousand – hence 22 carat gold consists of 907 parts of gold. Like 24 carat gold, it is extremely soft and is best used for chasing and embossing, or for the casting of small objects.

**18 carat gold (750/1000)** is usually light red or yellow, though, depending on the alloy, it can be deep yellow, red, orange-red, green-yellow, or even white in colour. The alloys used are fine silver, copper, nickel, or, in the case of white gold, zinc. The metal is widely used in jewellery making, as it is malleable and strong.

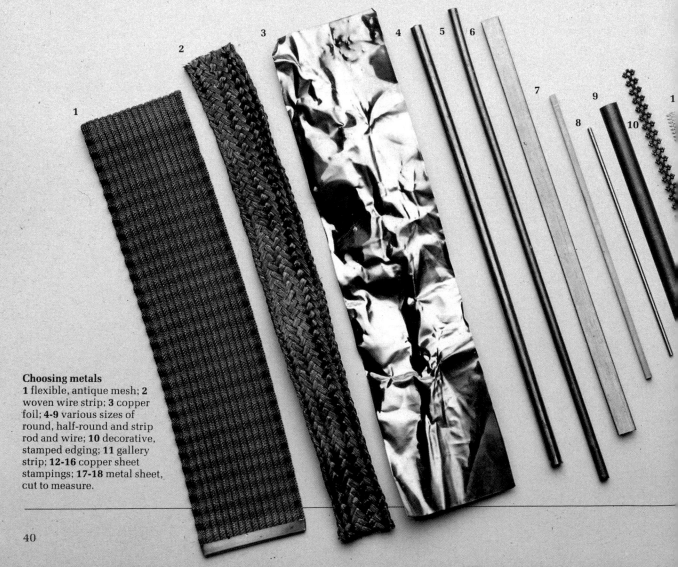

**Choosing metals**
**1** flexible, antique mesh; **2** woven wire strip; **3** copper foil; **4-9** various sizes of round, half-round and strip rod and wire; **10** decorative, stamped edging; **11** gallery strip; **12-16** copper sheet stampings; **17-18** metal sheet, cut to measure.

**14 carat gold (485/1000)** is green-yellow, pale yellow, dark yellow, red-yellow, red-orange or white, again depending on the alloy, which can be be fine silver, copper, nickel or zinc.

**9 carat gold (375/1000)** is red or yellow. It is used largely for mass-production jewellery, is quite hard, but discolours quickly when heated. It is the lowest quality of gold available.

Generally, pure silver is too soft to be used in jewellery making, though it is well suited to certain forms of decoration *(see below)*. To make it harder, copper is added to produce various grades.

**Fine silver** This is pure silver. It is soft and malleable and is ideal for repoussé work – in this decorative technique, you literally raise up your design and ornamentation three dimensionally from the flat metal sheet – chasing and embossing.

**Britannia silver (948.4/1000)** is alloyed with copper. Like fine silver, it is soft and malleable.

**Sterling or standard silver (925/1000)** is the commonest type of silver in general use. Again, it is mixed with copper. Though it is is extremely easy to work, you must take care not to over-heat it, or the copper will oxidize, with patches of copper oxide appearing on the surface as a result. This defect is known as fire stain. Generally, you can polish fire stain off the affected surface, but, in severe cases, the piece you are making may need silver plating to conceal the tarnish.

The other non-ferrous metals you may come across are copper, brass, gilding metal, pinchbeck (though this is largely of historical interest since it is not made today), nickel, nickel silver, bronze, so-called white metal, pewter and aluminium. Zinc is rarely used in itself, as it is too brittle to be worked, but it is present as an alloy in most of the metals listed here.

**Copper** is either 'hard' or 'soft'. When pure, it is a warm pinkish-red. It is malleable, ductile, easy to shape and handle and also comparatively cheap. This makes it an ideal material for you to use when starting your first jewellery experiments. Provided you ensure that the copper you are working is clean and fluxed, you can solder it with silver or lead solder.

Copper has two disadvantages, however. First, its softness makes it easy to bend or distort. Second, it tarnishes easily, so you should plate the finished surface, deliberately oxidize it with chemicals to produce attractive green, brown or black tones *(see p.124)*, or lacquer with clear metal varnish, though this will mar its natural warm beauty slightly.

**Brass** is an alloy of copper and zinc. It is stronger and harder than pure copper, while its colour depends on how much zinc it contains; it can vary from pale yellow to yellow.

**Gilding metal** is a form of brass, the difference being that it contains an extremely high percentage of copper and relatively little zinc. Its colour is a close approximation to gold, which is why one of its variants – pinchbeck – was used by 19th-century jewellers as an imitation gold.

**Nickel** is a hard greyish-silver metal commonly used in alloys. Because of its hardness, costume jewellers often use it to make chains, catches and links.

**Nickel silver** gets its name from its colour, which closely resembles silver; in fact, its constituents are copper, nickel and zinc. In its wire form, it is used in riveting and as the raw material for brooch pins.

**White metal** is a tin alloy, used to cast cheap costume jewellery. It is dirty white and very lightweight.

**Pewter** is the softest of the non-ferrous metals used in jewellery making. Basically, it is a tin alloy, with small additions of lead, copper and/or zinc, and has an extremely low melting point. It is well suited to embossing and also casts well.

**Aluminium** is light in weight and colour. It is most often used for costume and fashion jewellery, since it can be coloured in many different shades and also etched and stamped easily.

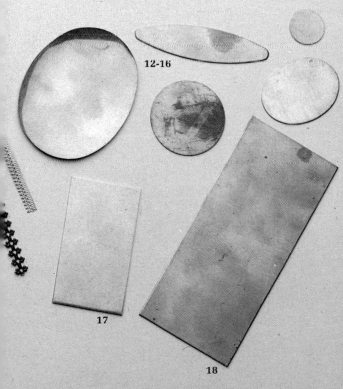

12-16

17

18

# Jewellery basics/2

### Ferrous metals

All ferrous metals contain iron.

**Cast iron** can be used in jewellery making, although it tends to be too brittle for fine work. The metal's main disadvantage is that it rusts and corrodes easily; in the 19th century, however, Berlin jewellers produced some beautiful cast iron work, which was protected from corrosion by a thick layer of black oxidization.

**Wrought iron** is low in carbon, soft and tough. Though it is not often used in jewellery making, it can be forged when hot or cold.

**Stainless steel** is iron-based, with a chromium and/or nickel content. It is highly resistant to corrosion and keeps a high degree of finish for a considerable length of time. Though it is difficult to solder, this can be done with high or low melting point solders. Modern jewellers frequently colour stainless steel pieces, giving them either a highly-polished or matt finish.

### Refractory metals

'Refractory' strictly means hard to melt or work. Such metals are divided into two groups – metals with high melting points (above that of iron) and light, low density metals. Examples of the former include titanium, niobium, tantalum, platinum, chromium, palladium, rhodium and their alloys; the latter include aluminium, magnesium and their alloys.

**Platinum** is the most expensive of the precious metals. This, combined with its extremely high melting point, makes it an unlikely material for you to use as yet; its hardness and lack of malleability also make it extremely hard to work. Professional jewellers use it in combination with gemstones, particularly diamonds.

**Chromium and rhodium** are generally used in plating. The former is used for cheaper pieces; rhodium has a brilliant finish and is used for plating white gold.

**Titanium, niobium and tantalum** are also expensive, so you should avoid their use until you are fully confident of your skills.

### Piercing, filing and polishing

Because metals are so important, it is vital for you to understand basic metal working techniques. Otherwise you will be unable to execute your designs.

### Sawing and piercing

For this, you will need a jeweller's saw. Together with a pair of pliers, this is the most essential of all tools, as the saw will not only cut metal, but also wood, shell, ivory and plastics. Buy one with an adjustable frame, as this will accommodate different lengths of blade. When you use the saw, always remember to hold it in an upright position, with the teeth of the blade facing down, as it is the down stroke, not the up stroke, as in woodworking, that actually does the cutting.

You can buy blades in bundles. The size of blade you will need depends on the thickness of the metal with which you are working, or the delicacy of your design. For intricate work, you will need a very fine blade (grades 8/0 to 3/0); standard blades are 2/0 and 1/0; coarse range upwards from 1 to 4. These grades are based on number of teeth per inch – the finer the blade, the greater the number of teeth. The thicker the metal you are working, the coarser the blade you need.

When fitting any blade, you must ensure it is fastened securely into the frame of the saw. Before you secure it, check that the teeth are facing downwards – this may sound like an over-obvious precaution, but it is one well worth taking. Secure the top end first by tightening the frame's top screws. Push the end of the frame against something solid – your work bench, for instance – and tighten the bottom screws to secure the other end of the blade. Check the final tension carefully. If you over-tighten the screws, the blade may well snap when you start to saw; if, on the other hand, the blade is too loose, it will bend as you saw and so you will lose control over the direction of the cut.

### Sawing out a design

You can mark out your design directly on to the metal with a sharp scriber; alternatively, trace it out on tracing paper and secure the trace in place over the metal with double-sided tape.

Decide the best place to start piercing and make a small notch there with a square or triangular needle file (*see below*). The purpose of the notch is to give the blade a chance to grip into the metal. Rub the blade

**Sawing metal sheet** Always hold the saw in an upright position and use long, even, downward strokes.

gently with a small block of beeswax before you start to saw – your aim is to get a little of the wax to stick to the teeth – as this lubrication will help to stop the blade sticking in the cut.

As stated previously, always hold the saw in an upright position, firmly gripping the metal you are sawing with one hand and the handle of the saw with the other. Saw in long, even strokes, using the full length of the blade. To turn corners, wiggle the blade up and down, at the same time turning the frame until the blade is facing in a different direction.

Do not despair if you break a few blades at first – as with any jewellery technique, perfect sawing takes practice. If you always remember to keep the frame upright, your blade should last a reasonable amount of time – sometimes until it is blunt, when it must be replaced.

### Files
There is a wide range of files available; the following are essential purchases. You will need a flat all-purpose file with a broad surface for trimming and bevelling edges and making straight joins. These files come in varying degrees of coarseness (No 2 cut is average).

A three-square file – this is a triangular file – enables you to shape angled corners. It can also be used on flat surfaces. A half-round file is essential for shaping the inside curves of items such as bangles and rings. The flat side can be used for conventional filing. For gentler curves, you will need a crossing file. This has two curved sides, the angles of the curves being less acute than those of a half-round file.

One of your most useful purchases will be a set of needle files, as these can reach areas that would otherwise be inaccessible. Though you can buy such files individually, a pack of a dozen is a good investment as the more you have, the better. For very fine work, you can use watchmaker's files, which are even smaller, or riffler files, whose ends are curved in various shapes. There are at least 18 different riffler tips you can buy.

### Getting down to filing
Practise filing on a square piece of metal first and then on a circular piece. Hold your work steady and file in long, even strokes, keeping the tool in continuous contact with the metal and grasping it firmly. Your wrist should control the movement. You will find your files easier to hold if you buy a wooden handle for them (one handle will fit all your files). The handle will also protect your hands.

Remember not to use the same file on different materials – it is particularly important to use uncontaminated files when working with precious

**Filing edges** File steadily, keeping your file in contact with the metal on the downward stroke.

metals, as the surface of the metal must be clean both for soldering and hallmarking (if desired). Reserve old files for use on plastic, steel and lead.

### Drilling
You will find a pendant drill extremely useful, although it is not an essential purchase. These drills are motor-powered and have flexible shafts; this means that the drill can be manipulated almost as easily as a drawing pen or pencil. As well as taking twist drills – the part of the drill that does the actual cutting – of various sizes, the chuck will also hold burnishers, small polishing wheels and other implements. You can regulate the speed of the drill as well, often through use of a foot pedal, just like a sewing machine.

What you will need is a good all-purpose electric drill, which you can either hold in the hand or clamp to a drill stand for intricate drilling. Such drills are extremely accurate. There are many different models available, some having additional refinements, such as adjustable speed controls and angled bases, all of which are reflected in their price. Buy the best you can afford.

For some work, a small hand drill may be required. To hold this, you will need a pin vice. This piece of equipment is easy to handle and extremely versatile, as it can be used to hold many different tools, from drills to fraizers (a type of burr used to enlarge or taper holes and also to texture metal surfaces) and burners. You will find, however, that this type of drilling takes time, as the twist movement it requires comes solely from your wrist.

# Jewellery basics/3

You will also need a centre punch to make a starting mark on the metal before you begin drilling it. You can buy one with an automatic action or a hand-held punch; if you choose the latter, you will also need a mallet to strike the punch.

## Practical drilling

Choose the type of drill best suited to the work in hand; this could be a pendant drill, a conventional electric drill, a hand drill, or, for small jobs, a pin vice. As stated above, you should use a centre punch to make a small indentation as a starting point first. The purpose of the indentation is to stop the drill from skidding or slipping and making unwanted and unsightly scratch marks on the surface you are working.

Naturally enough, the size of twist drill you choose depends on the size of hole required. If you are using an extremely fine twist drill, you will need to take extra care, as such drills can snap all too easily. Always make sure that your twist drill is firmly secured in the chuck, as otherwise it will wobble as you drill.

## Polishing

Achieving the best possible finish is one of the key jewellery skills you must practise. You start by dealing with the inevitable scratch marks that filing creates. These must be removed with emery paper. Start with grade three (the coarsest grade) and work through the others – 2, 1, 0, 0.1, 0.2 and 0.3 – finishing with rouge papers, all of which are very fine.

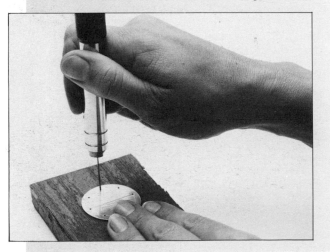

**Drilling with a pendant drill** Support your work on a wooden block and hold the drill in a vertical position.

Wrap a piece of paper around a flat or curved stick and smooth down, using the tool just as you would a file. You can reach awkward spots with a scrap of emery paper wrapped around your finger, or around a matchstick.

You can carry out the final polishing by hand, or by machine. Hand polishing involves working through all the available grades of emery paper, from the coarsest to the finest (see above). You then rub tripoli, a polishing compound, well into the surface with a clean cloth. Remove the tripoli with white spirit and then clean thoroughly in soapy water. For the final shine, apply rouge with another piece of soft cloth or cotton wool, removing the surplus with a soft brush and clean, soapy water.

As the above shows, hand polishing, though effective, is extremely arduous and time-consuming. For these reasons, you should invest in a polishing motor as a basic part of your jewellery equipment. You fit polishing mops of varying degrees of abrasion to the motor's spindle as required. You will need a felt mop for smooth, even surfaces, a bristle mop for textured or raised surfaces, a calico mop, which you use with tripoli for all-purpose polishing, and a soft wool or fine calico mop for use with rouge. A wire mop, made from steel or brass, can be used to get rid of scratches, while a useful extra is a felt ring cone for polishing the insides of ring shanks.

Whenever you use a wheel, you must take great care to hold your work firmly. If you slacken or loose your grip, the wheel's motive force might spin the piece of jewellery out of your hands, so damaging or breaking it. Always remember to clean off the tripoli before the final rouge polishing. You must also 'dress' a new cloth mop before using it – in other words, you must remove any over-long or loose threads.

Expert jewellers often find it worthwhile to invest in a barrell polisher. This is extremely useful if you are carrying out a great deal of polishing, particularly when dealing with costume or fashion jewellery. The machine consists of an electrically rotatable tank, filled with ball-bearings or shot, plus soapy water. These burnish the work as the tank rotates.

## Annealing and 'work hardening'

Annealing is one of the most important of the basic techniques. Particularly when working with sheet metal, you will find that the processes used in its manufacture result in the raw material becoming what is technically known as 'work hardened'. This means that the metal is harder than normal and so is difficult to shape and work. To restore it to its original state, you must anneal it; the process restores the metal's flexibility, so making it possible to bend or twist.

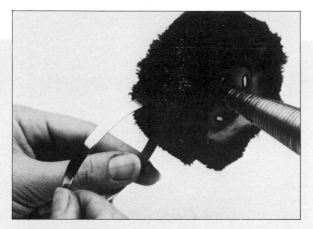

**Machine polishing** Hold your work firmly against the mop, turning it so that all parts are polished evenly.

You may also find it necessary to repeat the process as you work. This is because the stresses you set up in the metal by bending, hammering and twisting it will 'work harden' it again and, without annealing, the metal will ultimately fracture.

What you do is to heat the metal until it becomes malleable. When you do this, take care not to over-heat the metal – you are aiming to heat it until it turns dull red in colour – as otherwise you will damage it. You should also ensure that you apply heat evenly over the entire surface, or the metal may buckle. The thicker the metal, the longer it will take to anneal.

Depending on type, you should either allow the metal to cool naturally, or cool it quickly by quenching in water. Whichever the method, the aim is the same – to end up with a metal soft enough to work and shape.

To get used to working with the softened metal, experiment with the bending technique shown here. Use copper for this, as it is relatively cheap and naturally malleable. You will find that annealed metal can be bent, hammered and twisted into a multitude of attractive shapes – all ideally suited to jewellery.

'Work hardening', however, can be an extremely useful process in itself, especially if you are working with naturally soft metals. A pure silver brooch pin, for instance, might look extremely attractive, but it is unlikely that silver in its natural state could take the weight involved. If, however, you can twist the pin, you will harden it sufficiently to make its use viable.

## Pickling

One disadvantage of annealing is that the process often leaves a deposit of surface oxides on the metal, which can stain or even scale it. To remove stains or scales, you must pickle the metal – in other words, clean off the stain with a chemical solution. You may find it necessary to repeat the process several times as you create a particular piece of jewellery.

Generally, the main constituent of pickle is sulphuric acid, diluted with six to ten parts of water depending on the strength required. If you like, you can use a solution of powdered alum in water as an alternative. To make sulphuric acid pickle, you will need rubber gloves, a small glass or china dish – these must be heat resistant – a gas ring or hot plate, a piece of asbestos or asbestos-reinforced mesh and the acid itself. Place the dish containing the acid on the hot plate, protecting the base of the dish with the asbestos, and heat gradually. Do not allow the pickle to boil.

When the pickle is hot, carefully put the metal you are pickling into the solution with a pair of plastic tweezers. The acid will gradually lift off the oxidization. When the pickling is completed, wash the metal thoroughly in cold water and then dry.

Remember – working with acid always means observing basic safety rules carefully. For this reason, never forget about the acid and let it boil, since the fumes can be dangerous (in any case, the solution tends to evaporate naturally and, as it does so, is more likely to fume). Protect your hands and eyes and wear a protective coverall. If acid splashes on to your skin, rinse the affected area immediately with cold water. Avoid drips and splashes.

Do not pickle pieces containing lead, steel or iron, as the acid will react with them. You should replace the pickle when the acid turns a murky green, or grey/black when copper is immersed in it.

**Annealing wire** Heat the metal until it turns a dull red; it will then be soft and workable. If the wire becomes work hardened, anneal it again.

# Jewellery basics/4

### Doming
Another basic method that needs practise to perfect is doming. You use this technique to make circular depressions in annealed metal; it involves the use of a doming block and punch. The block itself is usually a square of brass or steel, with depressions of various sizes set into it; the punches come in sets, their sizes ranging from 2mm up to about 25mm. If you need a larger dome, make your own wooden block and buy a large wooden doming punch.

**Making a domed disc**
Pierce out a disc that will fit snugly into one of the depressions in a doming block. Anneal the disc. Using a heavy hammer, strike the matching punch into the depression, moving the punch evenly over the surface of the disc.

### Soldering
As every professional jeweller will tell you, the ability to solder correctly is vital. What you must understand from the start is why you solder; the aim is not to fill the space between the various components you are fixing together with a thick coating of solder, but rather to use as little solder as possible to make an almost invisible join. This means that the surfaces you are soldering must fit as closely together as possible before you start – you ensure this by filing them true – as otherwise the solder will not flow properly and the resulting join will be weak. For the same reason, the surfaces must be clean as well.

There are various grades of solder available, the grading system being based on the melting points of each individual solder. The common grades are hard, soft and easy – the harder the grade, the higher the proportion of the actual metal in the solder. Usually, you will be able to use hard solder throughout, but in

certain cases – if the piece of jewellery you are making is particularly complex, for instance – you may have to use various grades. In such a case, do all the hard soldering first.

Regardless of specific grade, all solders consist of two elements – a specific metal (gold in the case of gold solder, silver in the case of silver solder) and a proportion of a baser metal. The solder you use must be chosen to suit the metals you are soldering. When it comes to soldering gold, for instance, the solder should be of the same grade and quality as the gold itself; thus, if you are working with 18 carat yellow gold, the solder should be of the same colour and quality.

The exception to this general rule is silver solder. You can use this on base metals, such as nickel, brass or copper, if a strong join is required. It is also ideal for use on a piece which requires several solderings.

Both gold and silver solders come in the form of sticks or thin sheets, which you cut into very small pieces – these should not be much more than 0.5mm square – with shears or snips. Jewellers call these pieces 'paillons'. Keep them in a small airtight container until you need them and then position the individual pieces evenly along the join to be soldered, spacing them about 0.5mm to 2mm apart.

In addition to these two main solder types, you can use soft solder – this is sold on spools and can be fed into a join as the metal is being heated – when you are making costume or fashion jewellery. This is undoubtedly the fastest way of soldering, since the metals the solder contains all have low melting points. However, because they contain tin or lead, they should not be used to solder precious metals.

### Flux
No form of solder can be effective, however, without the use of flux. This keeps the items you are joining clean while they are being heated, prevents oxidization and helps the solder to flow. As with solders, there are various types of flux available; you should choose the one most suited to the specific solder you are using. You apply your chosen flux directly to the surfaces to be soldered, having heated the surfaces gently first.

With platinum, gold and hard silver solders, you use a special liquid antiflux, which is almost fluorescent green in colour. Ground borax, mixed with distilled water to form a milky paste, is suitable for use with most silver solders. Easyflow flux comes in powder form as well and is similarly mixed with water to form a paste. With soft solders, use bakers' fluid – you can buy this in most hardware stores.

Ideally, you should apply the flux with a special flux brush, though a small paintbrush can be used. Keep this clean by frequent rinsing in water.

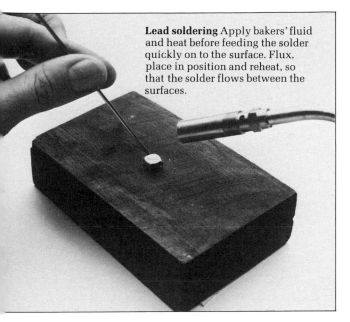

**Lead soldering** Apply bakers' fluid and heat before feeding the solder quickly on to the surface. Flux, place in position and reheat, so that the solder flows between the surfaces.

### Practical soldering – the golden rules
When you start to solder, remember the five golden rules. These are:
**1.** Gently warm your work before you apply the flux.
**2.** Remember that the flux plays just as crucial a part in the process as the solder itself. When you brush it on to the warmed surfaces, it should bubble gently and spread evenly. This even spreading is important, as it will help you to solder evenly.

Getting the temperature right is equally important. If the metal is too cold, the flux will dry patchily and will not penetrate the join as it should as a result. Its spread will also be uneven. If the metal is too hot, the flux will dry on contact, again with uneven penetration and coverage as the result.
**3.** Heat the work gently. Your aim is to get it hot, but not to change its colour.
**4.** Allow to cool slightly and then place the pieces of solder in position with a pair of tweezers, or with the tip of your brush. The solders you are using are ready-fluxed; this means that the cold flux they contain will amalgamate with the warm flux when the two come into contact, just like a glue.
**5.** Heat the join evenly. Immediately the solder flows, remove the flame.

### Soldering precautions
Soldering is not as difficult as you might first suppose, but the more you practise the more confident you will become. Before long, you will be able to judge exactly when solder will flow and how much solder to apply to a join. To aid in this, note these precautions.

Remember that it is important to apply an even heat over the entire area you are soldering and not a fierce, concentrated heat to any one part of it. If the heat is too fierce, the solder will form droplets, which may well fall off the piece; uneven heating, or the application of excessive heat to one side of a join, means that the solder may well flow away from the join to the hotter area, though, if this happens, you can use your tweezers to stroke it back again. Even heat means that the solder will flow into the join.

Calculating how much solder you will need in any given circumstance can also be a problem at the start. What you are aiming for is literally the smallest possible film of molten solder flowing between the surfaces you are joining. Remember that, when heated, solder will flow like water, so always start with slightly less than you think you will need; if you have underestimated, you can always add more and resolder.

If you have used too much solder, it will overflow the surface. If, on the other hand, too little has been used, it will not coat the entire surface as it should. You may be able to detect this visually as the solder melts, but, if not, the fault will be detected when the piece you are making is pickled and dried, as the process will reveal any gaps or cracks.

### Heat sources
In jewellery, you cannot use a conventional soldering iron as your source of heat – you will need a blow torch or a bottled gas torch as part of your basic kit of equipment. Blow torches are fitted with valves, which control the amount of gas flowing into the torch. They are also fitted with a second rubber or plastic tube, through which you physically blow. On its own, the natural heat of the gas would be insufficient for soldering; the air you blow is vital if the flame is to reach the requisite temperature. The latter work on the same principles, the only difference being that they are bottle fed.

Learning how to regulate the size and heat of the flame to suit the job in hand is something that comes with practice. Generally speaking, you can tell by sound when the flame is at its hottest. Do not blow too hard, or the flame will go out. For general soldering, you need a soft, bushy flame – to obtain this, turn the gas up to high and blow gently. For fine work – for the soldering of jump rings or links, say – you need a fiercer flame. This is likely to oxidize the surface, so you will have to pickle your work to remove the oxidization once the soldering has been completed.

When it comes to fine work, micro-welders can be useful, as they produce an extremely small flame. You vary the flame's size by attaching the appropriate torch tip to the body of the torch and then solder.

# Hollow silver hoop earrings

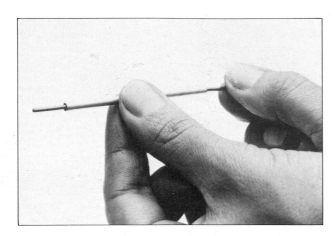

Because you are using silver tubing for this project, the size of the earrings can be varied to suit individual requirements – the medium and method is ideally suited to making fairly large ones.

One important point to remember is that you must protect the tubing from being dented when you bend and hammer it. You do this by threading wire through the tube. This should be well oiled and split into two, so that it can be easily removed. Leave small lengths of the thread wire protruding from each end of the tubing, so that you can pull it out easily.

**1** **Making silver hoop earrings** Cut two 7.5cm lengths of 3mm silver tubing. Oil a piece of wire, cut into two lengths and thread through the tube. ◀

**2** Anneal the tube (see p.45). Then gently bend the tube around a ring stake. Anneal again. Gently hammer out a circle with a mallet, leaving a gap of about 5mm. ▼

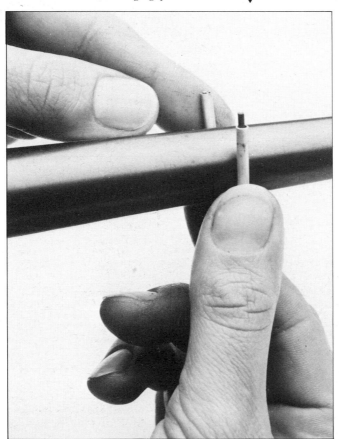

**3** Having shaped the circle, you can now discard the oiled wire you used to protect the tube while you were hammering it. Pull the wire out with a pair of pliers. If it sticks, pour a drop of oil into the tube to help you ease out the wire. ▼

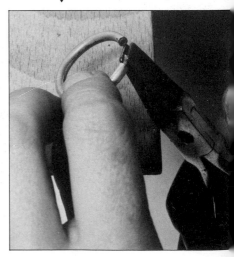

**4** File the end of the tube flat with an all-purpose file. Then file an angle on the ends to take the stud – your aim should be to set the stud at approximately 45° when you solder it. Smooth off with an emery stick. ▼

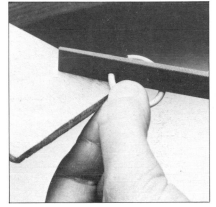

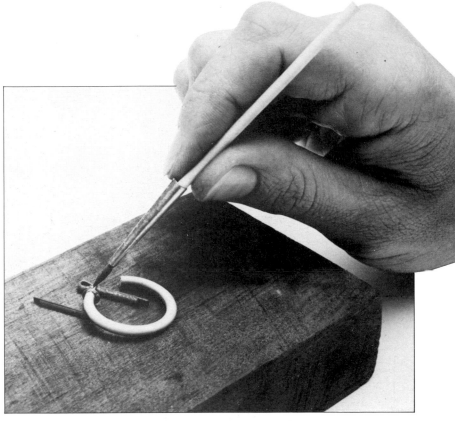

**5** Prop the stud in position with cotter pins and solder, using a generous amount of hard solder to make the join secure. Pickle (*see p.45*). Stand the tube in running water to remove all traces of acid. ▲

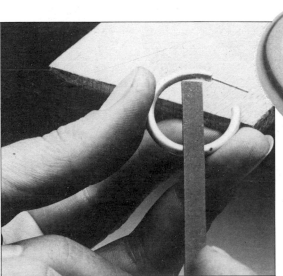

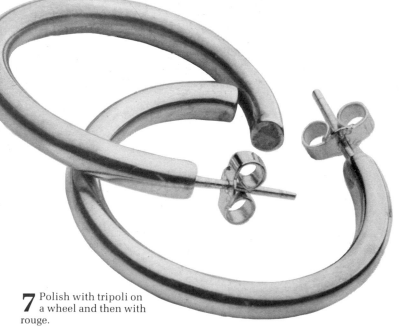

**6** Dry, file around the join until smooth and remove scratches with emery paper. You can leave the other end open or seal by soldering in silver wire. ▲

**7** Polish with tripoli on a wheel and then with rouge.

# Making a brass bangle

Metal bangles come in all shapes and sizes, but this basic technique can be adapted to suit any specific design or choice of material. You can alter the width of the bangle, for instance, or use another metal instead of brass. If you use brass as your basis, the finished bangle can be gold or silver plated, textured, coloured or oxidized.

It is advisable to make the bangle slightly larger than required to allow for inaccurate filing. The type of solder used is optional, but generally silver solder is preferable, even if you are working with base metals, as it is stronger and less messy than the alternatives.

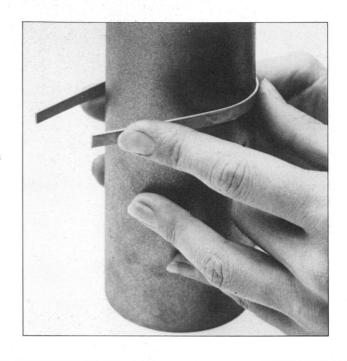

**1** **Making a bangle** Cut a 16-18cm long strip from a 1mm thick brass sheet. File the rough edges smooth. Anneal, pickle *(see p.45)* and wash. Bend the strip around a bangle mandrel, or a piece of metal tubing around 7cm in diameter. Tap the strip with a mallet until you have formed a circle. Do not tap too hard – if you do, you will create dents which you will have to remove. You can shape the strip until the ends meet, or, to allow for sizing, until they overlap slightly. ▶

**2** Make a true join with an all-purpose file. Hold the bangle carefully to prevent it from being pushed out of shape during filing and use steady, downward strokes. The angle of the join must be accurate if the soldering is to be successful. ▶

**3** Apply plenty of silver solder, so that the join will be invisible after filing. You can use lead solder, but I do not recommend it. If you do, remember that it does not need pickling and that you should use a separate file for the lead solder area. Pickle and wash. ▲

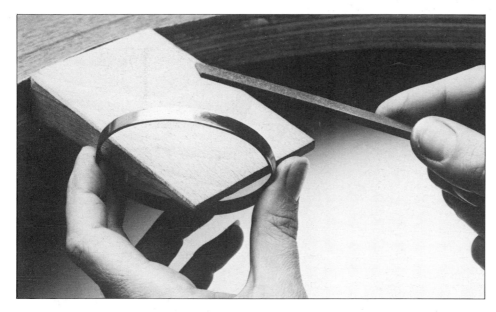

**4** File the soldered area smooth. To remove any scratches from the bangle, use a buff stick and different grades of emery paper, starting with grade 2 and continuing with 1, 0 and finally 02 until the surface is completely smooth. ◀

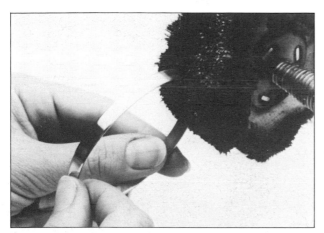

**5** Finally, polish the bangle on a wheel, first with tripoli and then with rouge. Hold it firmly against the centre of the wheel, turning it gradually until the whole surface has been polished. ▲

**6** Brass and copper bangles tend to leave green marks on the wearer's arm. Painting the bangle with lacquer will prevent this. Alternatively, you can have the bangle plated. ▶

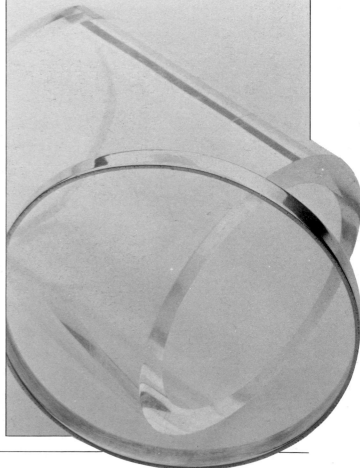

# Simple ring-making

I have used silver to make this ring but, when you have gained confidence, you can use exactly the same techniques to work in gold, substituting gold solder.

You will need 3mm half round silver wire, cut to length with a jeweller's saw. To establish the exact length you will require, slip your ring finger into a set of standard rings until you find the one that fits the best. Measure the internal diameter, halve it and multiply the result by 3.42. Add a little more to the result, so you have sufficient surplus to enable you to file a clean join. It is always better, too, to make the ring shank slightly too small, as it can be heated and tapped on a triblet to expand the metal and make the ring a little larger. If a ring is too large, you will have to cut out a piece of metal and resolder.

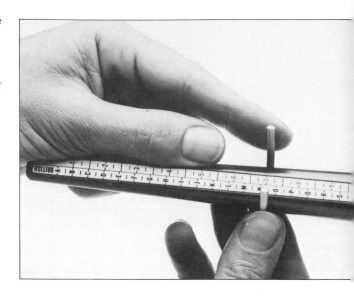

**1** **Making a ring** Anneal the cut wire until it is plum-coloured *(see p.45).* Gently bend the wire around a triblet with your fingers to get the size you require. ▶

**2** Anneal the shank again when the silver starts to feel less malleable. Gently tap it around the triblet with a mallet until a circle is formed. Remember that some metal will have to be filed away to make a fine join. I usually allow about 3mm, but the more accurate you are the less the wastage. ▶

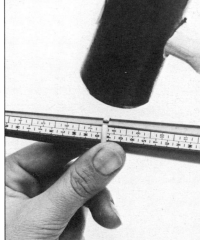

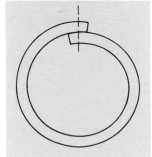

**3** Make a join by overlapping the ends of the wire and then sawing through them. If the angle is straight, very little filing will be necessary. ▶

**4** File the ends with a flat file until they mate exactly. This is important when it comes to soldering. ▲

**5** Cover the join with flux and apply three or four pieces of hard silver solder. Heat until the solder runs and the ring becomes red hot. Do not overheat, or the silver will melt. Allow to cool, pickle and wash. Replace the ring on the triblet and gently tap round the circumference, making sure that you do not dent the silver. If the ring is too big, cut down the solder seam with your saw and file to the correct size. ▶

**6** The join should be completely concealed by the solder and then filed smooth with an all-purpose file. Use a half round file on the inside, taking care not to make the ring larger by filing away too much metal. Remove any scratches by rubbing the surface carefully with emery sticks. ▼

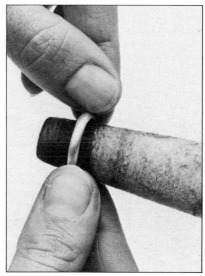

**7** Polish with tripoli on the wheel. Remove tripoli with white spirit. Brush dry and polish inside and outside the shank with rouge. ▲

# Basic settings

Through the ages, gemstones have been an integral part of jewellery making. At first, stones were simply drilled and strung into necklaces but, as metalworking skills became more sophisticated, various means of setting were devised. The essential function of any setting is to hold the stone securely. There are many methods of making a setting – the one you choose naturally depends on the size and shape of the stone to be set. However, the basic principle remains the same: the widest part of the stone, called the girdle, must rest on a level base, known as the bezel. It is vital to make sure that the stone is securely balanced and that the bezel is flat. If it is not, you may find that the stone tips unevenly or even fractures during setting. The area into which a stone is placed is known as the collet.

## Simple rub-over setting

This is a suitable type of setting for cut stones, such as cabochon. Essentially it is formed by fitting a narrow metal strip around the base of the stone, soldering the join and then pressing the top edge of the strip inwards with a setting tool until it grips the stone firmly.

The width of the strip depends on the height of the stone. It should be as narrow as possible, in order to display the stone to its full advantage, but wide enough to hold the stone in place.

A rub-over setting can be oval, round or square. It can also be decorated by piercing out the edge of the band to form a 'frilly' collet.

## Coronet or claw setting

A coronet or claw setting is based on a tapered collet and it is used for faceted stones. A simple form of coronet or claw setting can be made by using a collet plate and punch. The punch and plate are designed to turn a metal cylinder into a taper. Select a hole in the collet plate which is nearest to the size of the setting or, collet required. Place the cylinder in the hole and hammer the punch into it with a mallet. Once the collet is tapering at the correct angle, claws can be soldered to the outside of the collet. Alternatively, they can be pierced out of the collet itself.

If the claw setting needs a bezel, it is advisable to have the stone set professionally, as carving a bezel in a tapered setting requires considerable expertise.

## Wire collets

Wire can be used to make simple claw settings or, when you have more experience, elaborate and inventive designs. It is a suitable method for setting round stones of up to 8mm in diameter. Make two rings from round wire – one to support the stone just under the girdle and one to form the base. Make a claw setting by forming a cross, as shown, and solder it between the two rings. Saw out the centre of the collet, gently bend the claws up and trim them to length. Place the stone in the setting and push over the claws.

## Advanced settings

Stone setting is a highly specialized skill which requires formal training. Each type of setting has hundreds of potential variations, ranging from the simple to the extremely complex. If a stone has an unusual cut then the setting will have to be individually designed to accommodate the particular requirements of that stone.

Aside from rub-over settings and simple claw settings, it is preferable to select a suitable manufactured setting from the wide range available, rather than to attempt to make your own. Manufactured settings are either cast or stamped out, and they range from brass and gilding metal to silver, gold and platinum. However, if you have a particularly fine or unusual gemstone to set, it is advisable to have it mounted and set professionally, as incorrect setting may damage the stone.

## Grain setting

Grain settings are used to set clusters of precious stones. Because this is a delicate technique, requiring considerable skill, it is advisable to ask a professional jeweller to do it for you. The basic principle of the technique is that each stone is held in place by one or more tiny grains of metal. Metal shavings are scraped

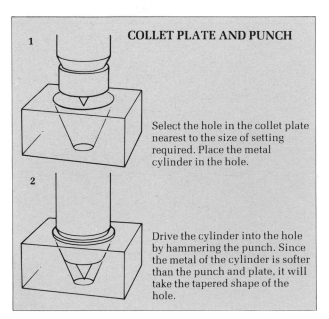

**COLLET PLATE AND PUNCH**

1

Select the hole in the collet plate nearest to the size of setting required. Place the metal cylinder in the hole.

2

Drive the cylinder into the hole by hammering the punch. Since the metal of the cylinder is softer than the punch and plate, it will take the tapered shape of the hole.

out of the metal collet, leaving a hollow for each stone. The stones must be firmly seated in their metal hollows before the shavings are rounded off to form grains and then pushed over the edges of the stones. These tiny grains are sufficient to hold the stones in their settings.

### Pavé setting
Pavé setting is another specialized technique best left to a professional jeweller. It is also used for setting clusters of stones but, unlike grain setting, the stones are clustered so closely that the metal grain setting is barely visible.

### Setting tools
Setting demands extra specialist tools. Setting tools have tips of varying shapes, which have been designed for specific tasks. There is a spit stick for cleaning the metal around stones after setting; a half-round scorper for raising grains from the metal collet; a ball stick for cutting bezels; a flat scorper for trimming claws and a pusher or a burnisher for pushing metal over the stones. You will also need setter's cement, which is used to hold the piece of jewellery in position while the claws, or rub-over setting, are being pushed over the stone and can then be burnt gently off the setting.

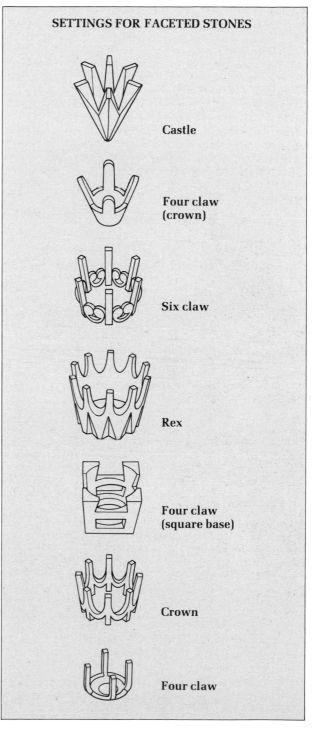

## SETTINGS FOR FACETED STONES

Castle

Four claw (crown)

Six claw

Rex

Four claw (square base)

Crown

Four claw

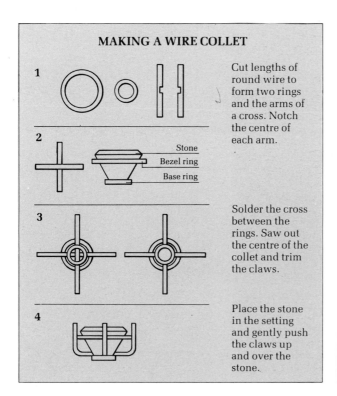

## MAKING A WIRE COLLET

1 Cut lengths of round wire to form two rings and the arms of a cross. Notch the centre of each arm.

2 Stone
Bezel ring
Base ring

3 Solder the cross between the rings. Saw out the centre of the collet and trim the claws.

4 Place the stone in the setting and gently push the claws up and over the stone.

# Stud earrings with 'cab' setting

These simple stud earrings can be made using any size and type of cabochon cut stone. I have chosen garnets set into silver.

You will need cabochon stones (in this case a pair of 5mm round garnets), an 0.25mm thick silver sheet for the settings, a 1.5mm strip of 0.9 mm thick silver sheet for the base and a pair of silver studs with butterflies. For the sake of economy, I suggest buying large sheets of 0.25mm and 0.9mm silver, as they are the standard sizes you will need for settings and bases.

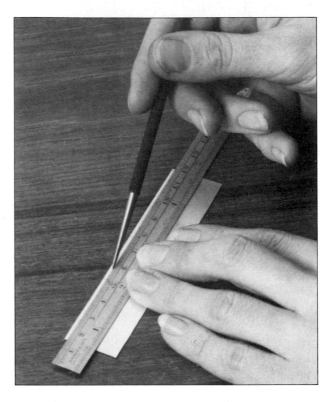

**1 Making stud earrings**
Use a fine blade to cut a strip of metal from the setting sheet long enough to go around the circumference of each stone, with a little over. The width of the strip should reach just above the point where the stone begins to taper. ▶

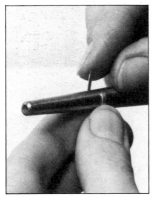

**2** Bend the settings round a small triblet. File the joins true with a needle file. Solder, heating gently and evenly. Replace each setting on the triblet and tap gently to shape a circle that will fit snugly round the stone. ▲

**3** The base sheet can be annealed and tapped flat with a mallet, or rubbed down with emery paper. The bases of the cabs should be rubbed flat with grade 1 or 2 emery paper. ▲

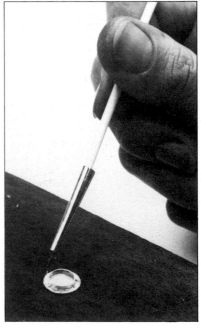

**4** Place the settings on the base. Position small pieces of solder evenly around the outside of the join. Solder, pickle and wash. ▶

**5** Saw around the setting, getting as close to the solder join as possible, but making sure you do not scrape it. File around the base until smooth. Emery until the silver shines. ▲

**6** Drill a central hole in the base. Place the stone in the setting to test for size and then push it out by inserting a pin through the hole. Smooth the base of the setting with emery paper. ◀

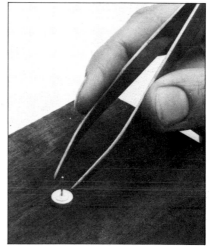

**7** Solder a stud to the centre of each setting with medium solder. Pickle and wash. You can solder a 0.9mm piece of silver wire into the hole, or buy a flatbacked stud. ▲

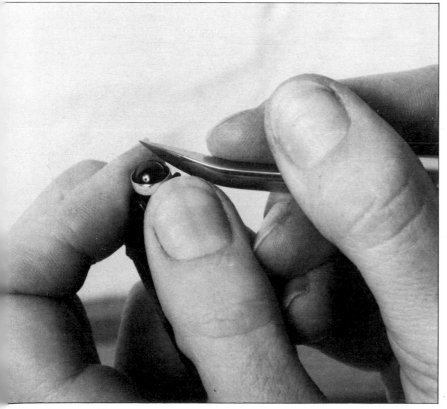

**8** Make sure that the stone sits flat in the setting. Push the setting over the stone with special setting tools or with a burnisher, turning the earring carefully but firmly and easing the metal over the stone. Gradually the collet will grip the stone. Make sure that the edge is smooth. Then polish. ◀

# A ring with a 'cab' setting

This type of setting, known as cabochon, was particularly popular in Victorian times. Butterfly wings, pictures, silks, and gold or silver leaf were set under glass or rock crystal so that they shone through the clear settings. I have chosen to set a cabochon stone on a wire ring shank, but you could use a shank made from sheet.

You will need approximately 12cm of silver wire, a strip of silver for setting, clear cab cut quartz, butterfly wings, silver for the base of the setting and cotter pins. Cotter pins are used to clamp metal together and to keep it in place while soldering.

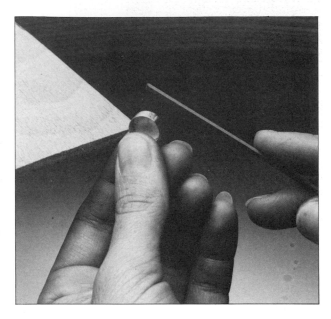

**1** **Making a ring with a 'cab'setting** Make a setting, following the instructions on page 56. Drill the centre with a 0.8-0.9mm drill. Next, construct two rings of the same size from the silver wire *(see p.52)*. ▶

**2** Solder the rings together at the base of the shank, using cotter pins to hold the tops of the rings 1cm apart. The soldering must be accurate, or the setting will not balance correctly. Pickle *(see p.45)* and wash. ▲

**3** Solder the setting to the exact centre of the top of the shank with medium or easyflow solder. The ring shank can be kept upright with spring tweezers or cotter pins. Pickle and wash again. ▶

**4** File with an all-purpose file and give the surface a final smooth with emery paper wrapped around your fingers. Hand rubbing helps you to retain the circular shape. ▲

**5** Use a scalpel to cut out selected areas of the butterfly wings very delicately and carefully, taking care not to rub off the dust which forms the decorative colour. ▲

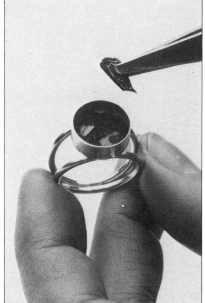

**6** Arrange the sections of butterfly wing in the collet and secure, using a mild all-purpose glue. ▲

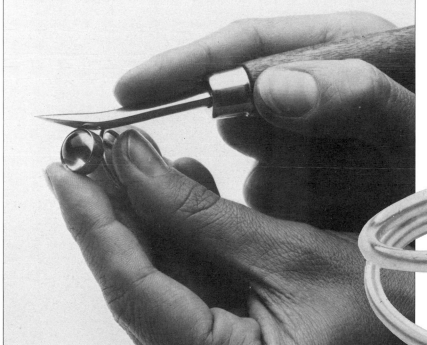

**7** Place the quartz securely in position and set (see p.56), holding the ring firmly. Polish, making sure that the piece does not become wet, or the butterfly wings may become discoloured. ▲

Cabochon is an attractive, yet unusual, type of setting, which you can use in various ways to add individuality and style to your jewellery.

# A string of beads

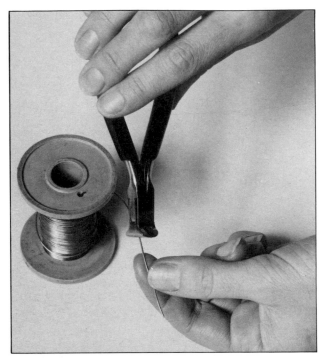

T his basic technique for stringing beads can be adapted to a variety of different styles. Copper wire can be replaced by gold or silver wire; ceramic or wooden beads, or semi-precious stones, or combinations of each can be used instead of the glass beads shown here.

You can alter the length of the necklace, and the size of the beads or stones, to suit your own taste. Shorter lengths of strung beads can be also used for bracelets, or attached to clips for earrings.

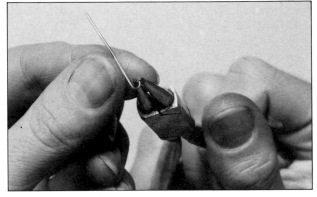

**1** **Making a necklace** Use snips to cut 2.5-cm (1-in) lengths from gauge 11 copper wire – one length for each bead. If this gauge of wire will not thread easily through your beads, use a smaller one.

**2** Hold one end of a length of copper wire firmly in one hand and, gripping the other end with a pair of round-nosed pliers, bend it around the end of the pliers. You are aiming to form a small loop.

**3** Flatten the loop carefully with a pair of parallel pliers. (This will create a neat finish to the necklace.) Thread the bead on to the wire.

**4** Trim the open end of the wire to about 6mm (¼in) with your snips. Bend the wire as before, and flatten the loop. Repeat the entire threading process with all the beads.

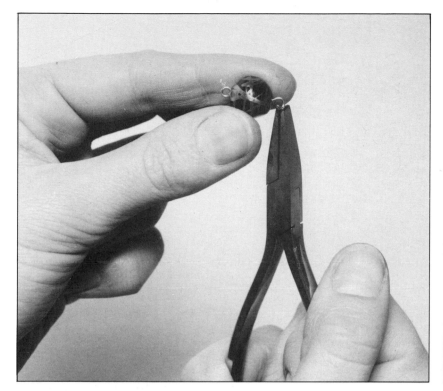

**5** To join the beads, first gently half re-open the loop at one end of a threaded bead.

**6** Slip the loop of another threaded bead inside the opening. Then close the link firmly, using a pair of all-purpose pliers.

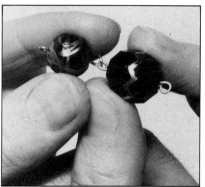

**7** Continue the linking process, bead by bead, until you have joined enough beads to make a necklace of the length you require.

**8** Fit a commercial catch to join each end of the necklace. This can be linked up in the same way as the individual components themselves.

# Openwork earrings/1

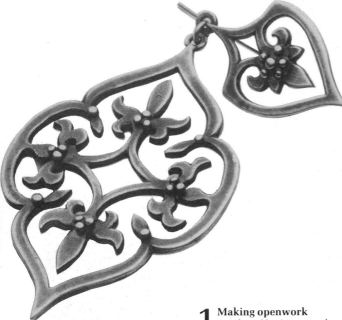

These earrings show just how other cultural images can influence jewellery design.

The design of these earrings is inspired by the Moorish architecture of the Alhambra in Spain. If you like, you can vary their dimensions, or use stones instead of granulation.

You will need a 5 x 9 cm piece of 1mm thick brass or silver sheet. To enhance the three-dimensional effect, use slightly thicker sheet and then bevel the edges. You will also need 1 mm round wire, silver ear wire about 0.8 to 0.9mm thick and six jump rings.

In the case of an intricate design like this, it is advisable to trace it on to graph paper. Fix the pencil tracing with artists' fixative, or hairspray, as otherwise the friction that is created by the piercing process might rub off the design.

**1 Making openwork earrings** Having traced out the design, fix the tracing paper to the metal sheet with double-sided tape. ▶

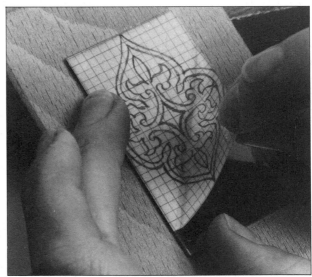

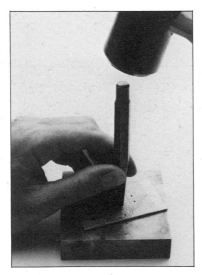

**2** With a centre punch and a mallet, mark the metal at points well within the outline of the pattern. ▲

**3** Drill holes where you have marked the metal. Use a pendant drill and a 1mm bit. ▲

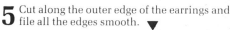

**5** Cut along the outer edge of the earrings and file all the edges smooth. ▼

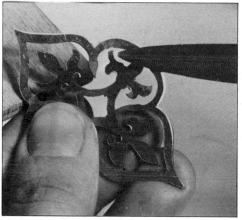

**4** Loosen the bottom screw of the saw, thread the blade through one of the holes and tightly reattach it. Hold the piece firmly, keep the blade upright and saw steadily, making sure that you follow the design accurately. Repeat until you have sawn out the complete design. ▲

**6** Use needle files to smooth all the jagged edges of the openwork. Cut very small pieces of 1mm silver wire into lengths of about 1-2mm for the granulation. Heat each piece with a blow torch until it melts into a tiny sphere. ◄

**7** Mark out the arrangement of the granulation with a centre punch. Apply flux and position the spheres. Tuck small pieces of hard silver solder close to their outer edges. Heat slowly, pickle (see p. 45) and wash. ▲

# Openwork earrings/2

**8** Solder a jump ring to each earring at the point where they are to be suspended. Make the upper portions of the earrings, following steps 1-7. ▶

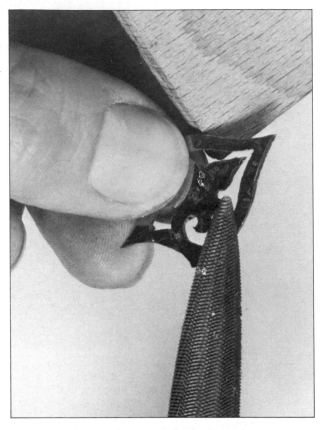

**9** Cut two 4cm lengths of silver ear wire. Place one end of each wire on a steel block and flatten them slightly with a hammer. Alternatively, the ends can be flattened in a rolling mill. ▶

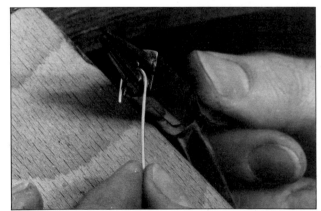

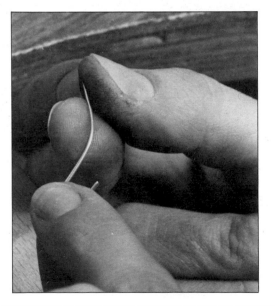

**10** Leaving the hammered part flat, curve each wire around with roundnosed pliers. The flat area ensures a stronger join when it is soldered to the top portion of the earring. ▲

**11** The tail part of the ear wire looks better with a gentle curve – the best way to do this is to shape it with your fingers. File the ends of the ear wires until they slip smoothly through the lobe of your ear. ▶

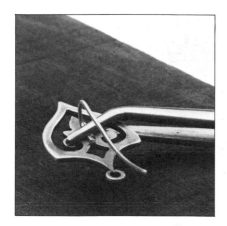

**12** Solder the ear wire to the top part of the earring. Hold in place with spring tweezers and use easyflow solder. Pickle and wash. Smooth down any uneven surfaces with emery paper wrapped around your fingers. ▲

**13** Polish with a calico tripoli mop on a wheel. Hold the work firmly, particularly the top part which will be more difficult to polish because of the ear wire fitting. ◀

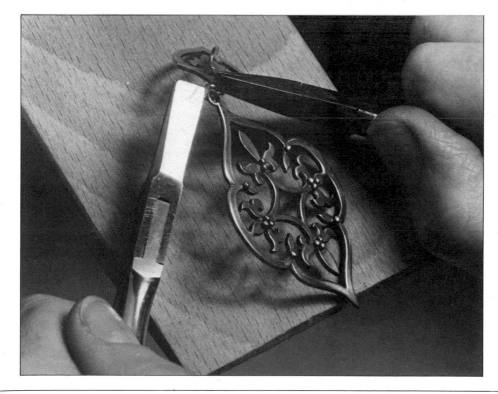

**14** Link the two parts of the earring together, using pliers and a small jump ring. Remove all traces of the tripoli with white spirit and polish with rouge. Silver plating and oxidizing are optional extras. ◀

# Casting

Casting is an ancient technique, its origins dating back about 5000 years. It is used to reproduce identical copies from a single original master model, or to produce a shape which would be difficult to achieve by using any other method. The basic technique involves making a hollow mould of the original piece and pouring molten metal into it. When the metal has solidified and the mould is removed, a replica of the original object will be produced. The mould can be made from a variety of materials, ranging from cuttlefish bone to clay, rubber or a special type of plaster, called investment plaster.

Though you can make your own model out of metal or wax, this is as far as you should take the process as an amateur. Leave the actual casting to a professional. Melting metal is difficult and it can be dangerous. In addition, professional castings are much more finished. Once your piece has been cast, you can then add the finishing touches.

## Cuttlefish casting
Cuttlefish bone casting is the simplest of the casting methods, but you should not attempt it unless you feel confident about handling molten metal. Cuttlefish casting is only suitable for reproducing one copy of a hard object and it should not be used to reproduce fine detail. You will need two cuttlefish bones, or charcoal blocks, some lengths of wire to use as pegs and some coarse sandpaper.

Smooth the flat surfaces of the cuttlefish with sandpaper. The two surfaces must fit accurately, otherwise the molten metal will leak out of the mould. Press your model firmly into one of the cuttlefish bones until it is embedded half way and then press the other cuttlefish on top of it. Alternatively, carve half of your design into each cuttlefish. To ensure that the halves fit together exactly, embed pieces of wire in the corners of the bottom cuttlefish, leaving the ends of the wire projecting upwards. Now force the top bone on to the wires. When you are satisfied with the fit of the two cuttlefish, remove the model and carve a channel from the edge of the cuttlefish bone to the edge of the impression. This channel is called a sprue; it allows molten metal to pass into the mould to form a cast.

Coat the impression with a fine oil and bind the two cuttlefish bones together with wire. Silver is the easiest metal to use when cuttlefish casting since it is relatively clean and casts well. Heat the silver (see p.109) and then pour the molten metal into the sprue. Allow it to solidify and remove the cuttlefish bones.

## 'Lost wax' casting
This is a sophisticated casting technique, which is used to reproduce very fine, intricate work. In this method of casting, the model is made in metal, or wax. If your model is made of metal, you will need to make a rubber mould of it so that your design can be reproduced in wax. The wax replicas can be arranged to form a 'tree' by attaching them to a central wax trunk by their sprues. This wax tree is placed upright in a can, which is then filled with investment plaster. The wax is melted out and the cavity is filled with molten metal.

Alternatively, you can carve your model directly out of wax. Dental wax makes ideal modelling material as it can be carved easily, either with engraving tools or with warm knives. The specific type and form of dental wax you choose will depend on your requirements and it is best to discuss the possibilities with the casters before you buy any. Because dental wax is a very pure wax it will not leave any impurities in the mould.

## Sprues
One of the most important aspects of any casting is the positioning of your sprue. A simple design may need only one sprue, while a more complicated piece may need three or four. The sprues can be straight or curved and should be arranged so that the metal flows smoothly into every part of the design. Multiple sprues should be positioned evenly around the design so that they meet in a central sprue. If you are in any doubt about where to place your sprues, it is advisable to consult professional casters. Solder the sprues to the piece with hard solder, as lead solder will melt during the casting process. When castings return from the casters, the sprues must be sawn off and the edges filed clean.

## Rubber moulds
Rubber moulds are used to produce large numbers of an individual item. The moulds are permanent, very flexible and capable of reproducing fine detail. It is useful to know how to make rubber moulds, although it is easier to have them made by professional casters.

**Removing sprues** Use snips to remove small sprues and a saw for larger ones.

Various types of rubber can be used to make moulds, but all of them have to be mixed with a suitable chemical reactor, which acts as a setting catalyst. If you are using silicone rubber, it is particularly important to follow the mixing instructions carefully, or the rubber will not set correctly. Mix the rubber and chemical reactor together and stir thoroughly. It is essential to work in a well-ventilated area, to keep food and drink away from the silicone and to make sure that the rubber does not get into open cuts or into your eyes.

Take your original metal design and sprue it, or if you prefer, take it to the casters to be sprued. Coat the design and sprue with parting agent and press them into a block of plasticine until they are set half way into the block. Build plasticine walls around the embedded piece and coat the inside area and model with a parting agent. Fill the walled area with rubber compound and allow it to set. When the top half of the mould is set, remove the walls and take your model and its mould out of the plasticine. To make the other half of the mould, invert the model, replace it in the plasticine and repeat the process. When the rubber has set, separate the two halves. Check that the sprue hole is clear. The mould is now ready for filling with hot wax.

### Advanced casting

Centrifugal casting, vacuum casting and gravity casting are used extensively by manufacturing jewellers and professional casters but, since all these methods require expensive equipment, they will not be used by the amateur jeweller.

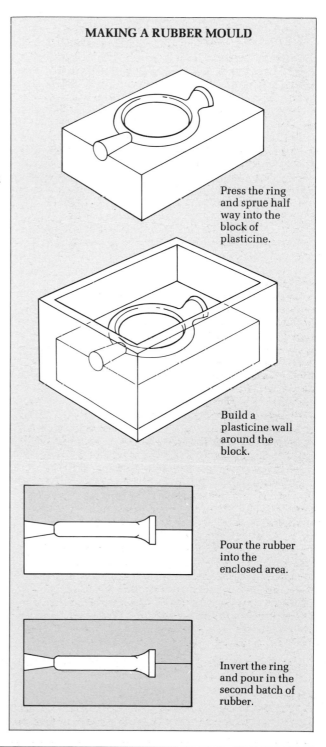

**MAKING A RUBBER MOULD**

Press the ring and sprue half way into the block of plasticine.

Build a plasticine wall around the block.

Pour the rubber into the enclosed area.

Invert the ring and pour in the second batch of rubber.

---

### POINTS TO REMEMBER

**1.** As metal cools in a mould, it will shrink by an amount that will vary from 2 to 10%, depending on the caster. Ask your caster how much shrinkage you can expect and then make your model slightly larger than the size required.

**2.** Sprues must be correctly positioned, as metal will not flow contrary to the main flow of metal. Ask the caster for advice.

**3.** Sprues must be soldered on with hard solder.

**4.** When castings return from the casters, the sprues must be snipped or sawn off and filed clean.

**5.** The surface of the metal may need polishing with emery paper.

**6.** Remove burrs with a scalpel, or with a file.

**7.** Holes are best drilled after casting.

**8.** Some shapes are difficult to cast, so the caster may tell you to change the position of your sprues, or to modify your design.

# Casting simple designs

Casting is a labour-saving method of reproducing identical units. Because the equipment is expensive and highly specialized, few jewellers do their own casting, but, like them, you can design and prepare your master mould and then take it to a professional caster.

Trace the design for the component you want to cast on to gridded tracing paper and, using doublesided tape, fix it to a piece of 2mm thick brass sheet. Cut around the edge of the design with a fretsaw. To cut out the inner design, mark appropriate points with a pencil and then drill holes. Fit your jeweller's saw with a fine blade, slip through each hole and, holding the piece firmly, saw out your pattern.

**1** **Making a simple cast design** Remove the tracing paper. Using a flat file on the outer edges and a needle file on the inner edges, file and bevel all the edges of the component. ▶

**2** Snip off a few short pieces of silver wire and heat them with a soldering torch until they form tiny uniform spheres. The pieces of wire should be small and of equal length, or blobs will form instead of spheres. ▼

**3** Arrange the spheres on the component and solder them into position, using hard silver solder. Add a jump ring to the base of the component, opening it slightly so that it fits round the tip. Solder it in place. Pickle (see p.45). ◀

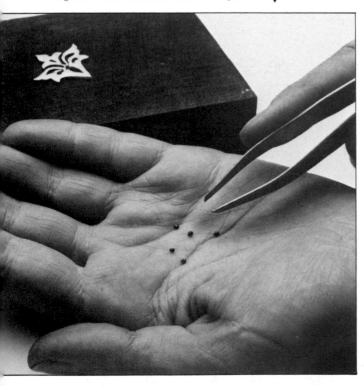

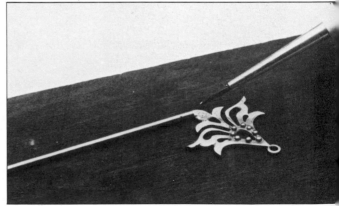

**4** To form a sprue (see p.66-7), solder a length of 2-3mm thick brass rod to the top of the component, as shown. Use silver solder, as lead solder will melt during casting. Polish before sending the piece to professional casters. ▲

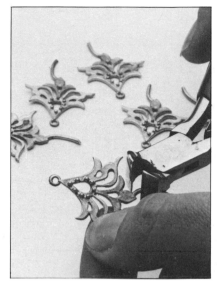

**5** When the casters return the components, you can either clip off the sprues with snips, or remove them with a saw. Rough areas should be filed smooth and any surface bubbles scraped off with a scalpel. ▲

**6** Choose a suitable piece of chain, 35-38cm long, and attach your components to it at suitably spaced intervals. Use all-purpose pliers to fasten the jump rings securely to the links. ◀

**7** Using all-purpose pliers, attach a catch to one end of the chain and a large jump ring to the other end. A bolt catch is best, but you can use another type if you prefer.

The finished necklace shows how casting can be used to reproduce as many simple shapes as you require, so saving hours of repetitive labour.

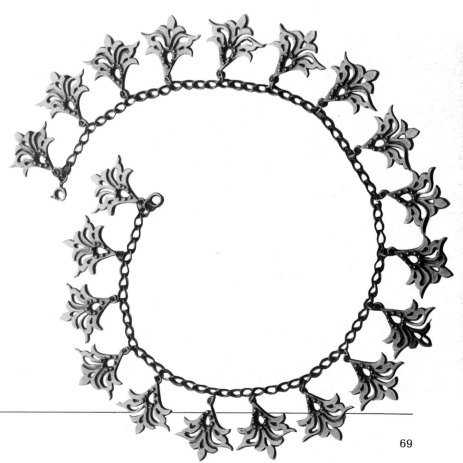

# Links, catches, fastenings and chains

Jewellery catches, fastenings and links are known as findings. When you first start making jewellery, you will find it easier to buy them, rather than to attempt to make your own.

Since bought findings are mostly machine-made, they can vary considerably in quality. It is a false economy to buy very cheap findings, as they are apt not to work at all or else to break after a short period of time. Whatever quality you decide on, however, you should study your design and decide what type of fitting would be appropriate in terms of function and appearance, before selecting findings from the vast range available. If you were to attach a tiny, delicate catch to a chunky necklace, for example, it would not only be unable to support the weight of the necklace, but it would also look unattractive.

When you have some more experience you should think about making your own components. Though the task is intricate and skilled, it is very satisfying. A hand-made fastening will almost certainly function more effectively than a bought one; this is particularly true of brooch catches and pins. In addition, the craftsmanship of the findings will then be comparable to that of the piece itself. If you would rather not spend time making findings for a particular piece, it is possible to modify bought findings by adding stones, or by soldering on decorative devices.

I suggest that you start by making ear fittings, as these are fairly simple and quick to make. Always use silver ear wire, even if your earrings are made of base metal, as some people are allergic to nickel.

## Chain

It is possible to make your own chain, but this is very time-consuming and, considering the wide range of chain available, neither practical nor economic. There are workshops that specialize in hand-made chain, but this is very expensive. It is only worth using for very special, or very valuable, pieces of jewellery.

Machine-made chains are available in gold, platinum, silver and base metals in a variety of designs and shapes, as you can see from the selection of chains illustrated. However, because there is less demand for fancy brass and copper chains than for precious metals, it is becoming increasingly difficult to find them. Keep an eye out for old chain in junk shops. If you would like to make some simple chain, the easiest method is to link jump rings together, either singly, or in pairs. Alternatively, wind wire around a jig – a design formed by driving nails into a block of wood – and then link the shapes. Once you have a short length of chain, test its strength by tugging it. If any of the links come apart, you will have to solder each one, which explains why it takes so much time to make chain.

**BASIC FINDINGS**

**Earring fittings**

for pearl or bead stud

for pearl with drop

for larger pearl or bead

for drop or charm

pierced ear fitting for charm or drop

pierced ear fitting for charm or drop, with safety mechanism

flat based studs

rivet clip fitting

squeeze clip fitting

bolt ring catch for chains

butterfly for ear stud

screw earfitting for pearl or bead

pearl or bead drop fitting

pendant fitting

drop fitting

**Catches**

chain and necklace catches

barrel catch

fancy snap catch for chain

box catch

all-in-one brooch fitting

brooch safety catch

hinges for brooch

**Stampings**

gallery strip

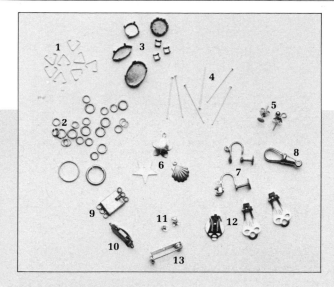

**Assorted findings**
1 triangular links for drilled drops; 2 jump rings; 3 base metal claw settings for paste; 4 pins to secure beads, etc; 5 posts with butterfly screws for stud earrings; 6 decorative stampings; 7 screw-earring fittings; 8 watch fob catch; 9 base metal box catch; 10 snap catch; 11 hinge and catch for brooch back; 12 clips for clip earrings; 13 bar brooch back used for wood and plastic, where soldering is not possible.

**Types of chain**
1 trace chain; 2 rope chain; 3 filed curb chain; 4 ball chain; 5 loop the loop chain; 6 snake chain; 7 box snake chain; 8 small rope chain; 9 small Prince of Wales chain; 10 large trace chain; 11 medium Prince of Wales chain; 12 rolled curb chain; 13 large curb chain.

# A simple silver chain

This basic chain-making technique can be varied by choosing different types of silver tubing – any size and length can be used – though you could use silver wire and silver balls as alternatives if you like.

Whatever raw material you select, however, the technique remains essentially the same. Here, I have chosen 2.5 mm tube cut into 1.5cm lengths, 0.8mm silver wire, drilled silver balls with a diameter of 2.5mm and 0.9mm wire for the hand-made 'S' catch.

**1 Making a silver chain** Cut the tube into 1.5cm lengths. The number of pieces required will depend on the length of the chain. ▶

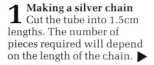

**2** File the ends of the tube flat and then smooth them with emery paper. Use snips to cut the silver wire into 4cm lengths and anneal them (see p.45). ▶

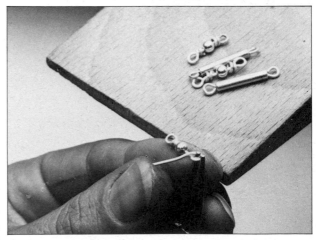

**3** With roundnosed pliers, make a loop at one end of each wire, 1.2-3 cm from the tip. Continue to hold the wire with the pliers and wrap the excess wire neatly around the base of the loop. Thread wire through each piece of tube and loop the other end with the pliers. ▶

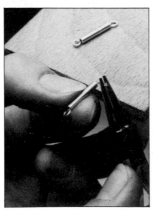

**4** Thread a silver bead. Make loops as before and twist the wire to secure the bead. Tidy the ends with a needle file. Make eight to ten of these. ▲

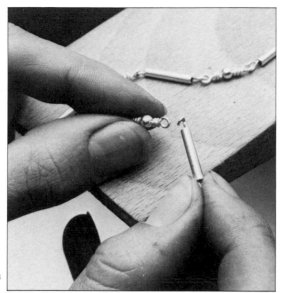

**6** This attractive 'S' catch is often found in oriental jewellery and is easy to make. Shape an elongated 'S' from 0.9mm wire, using roundnosed pliers. ▼

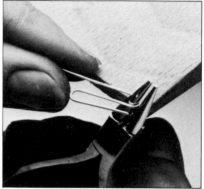

**5** Link the necklace components, using roundnosed pliers gently to re-open the loops at one end of the tubes, and thread them together loop to loop. ▶

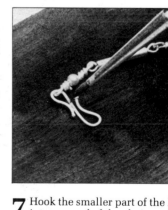

**7** Hook the smaller part of the loop into one end of the chain and solder it at the point where the end meets the curve of the 'S'. A decorative touch can be added by melting the tips of the 'S' to form a ball. ▲

You could wear this chain as a necklace, or use it as a decorative watch chain, as here, buying a silver fob catch to put on the other end.

# Bracelet with crystal decoration

When you make this bracelet, remember that the linking system is crucial, as there must be sufficient flexibility to allow the bracelet to curve easily around the wrist. The degree of flexibility depends on accurate measuring. If the links are marginally too long, or if the circles are too wide, the bracelet will not fit correctly. For this reason, it is best to experiment and test before finally linking the components together to form the finished bracelet.

You will require brass sheet (1mm thick for the doughnut shapes and 0.5-0.8mm thick for the links), silver wire for granulation, faceted crystal stones, 8mm in diameter, and readymade brass claw collets.

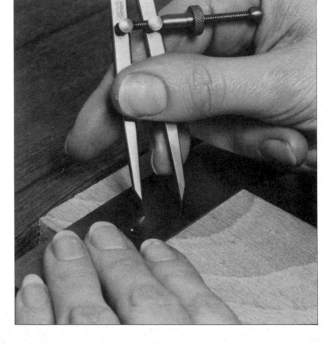

**1** **Making a bracelet with crystal decoration** Using dividers, mark out the doughnut shapes (circles with holes in the middle). For this bracelet I have used eight alternate sizes of ring approximately 2cm and 1.5cm in diameter. Ring width should be 3-3.5mm. ▶

**2** Drill out the centres, cut out the centre circle and then the outer. File the coarse edges smooth, using a round file for the inner circle and an all-purpose file for the outer. Create the granulation (see p.62) – make sure that you leave a gap in the pattern for the linkage – and solder. ▲

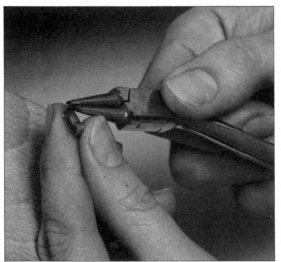

**3** To make the links, cut out strips of thin brass approximately 2.2cm in length and 3mm wide. File and smooth the edges. Anneal (see p.45). Find the centre of the strips and bend each one around the tip of the pliers to form half a square. Anneal again. Then bend the ends with round nosed pliers to form the links.

**4** Place the brass collets upside down on a charcoal block and heat very gently, removing the collets from the heat before the metal changes colour. Apply baker's fluid (see p.45). Heat again for about five seconds and then touch the lead solder to the hot collet, dropping the link in place as the solder flows. ▲

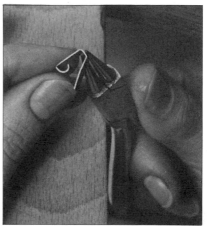

**5** After soldering each link, brush it clean with washing-up liquid. Open each link with round pliers until you can slip two circles on to it. Slip the circles on to each link in turn and then close it. ▲

**6** For the catch, anneal a 2.5cm strip and bend it slightly off centre with parallel pliers. Bend the short end as in step 3, and the other end over a stake until just concave. ▶

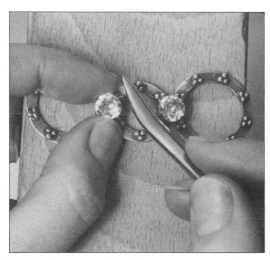

**7** Drop the faceted crystal into the collet. Hold it in place with one hand and push over the claws with a burnisher until the stone is held securely. Carefully solder the catch to the last link of the bracelet with lead solder. ▲

**8** When you have finished making the bracelet, you can have it silver plated and oxidized. You can substitute coloured stones for the crystal if you like. ▶

# Bar brooch

There are many ways of making a simple bar brooch. Here, I have used two lengths of 1.5mm silver wire – these you solder together to form the bar – an oval snowflake obsidian in a rubover setting and two little claw-set pieces of jet.

You will need 1.5mm silver wire, two bought settings for faceted stones, 4mm in diameter, one oval black snowflake obsidian, brooch fittings and 'hardenable silver' wire for the brooch pin.

Cut the silver wire into two equal lengths of 5-6cm. Straighten by annealing and tapping flat with a mallet on a steel block. Solder the two pieces together with pieces of hard silver solder, placed 2-3mm apart.

**1 Making a bar brooch** If you do not have an oval stake, you can make a template from a wooden stake or rod. Cut a strip of thin silver sheet (0.5-1mm thick) long enough to go around the perimeter of the stone with a bit to spare to allow for fitting and filing. Make sure that the strip is the right length before continuing. ◀

**2** Anneal the strip of silver and bend it around the stake. Remove, solder the ends and replace it to check that you have a good oval and to let the silver harden. The setting should fit snugly around the stone. Check this carefully. ▼

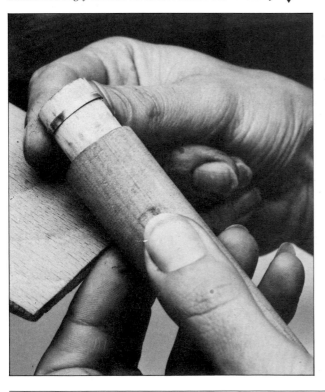

**3** Smooth the base flat with emery paper and solder the setting to it. Pickle (see p.45). Saw closely around the setting, file and smooth with emery paper. ▲

**4** Place the setting upside down on a charcoal block and centre the bar. Use hard silver solder, removing the heat as soon as the solder flows. Cool and pickle. Then turn the brooch the right way up. Solder on the two little settings either side of the oval. ▲

**5** Solder on the brooch fittings – a hinge with a hole for riveting the pin into and a bolt catch for the tip. Use the same solder as in step 4, but take care not to use too much as an excess could jam the mechanism. Take care not to overheat as well, since this could melt or break the fittings. ▲

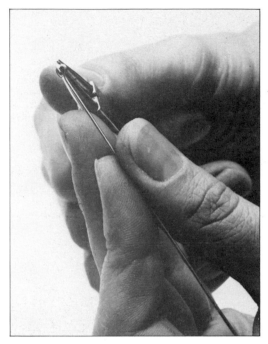

**6** Make a pin from 0.75mm hardenable silver wire. Use round-nosed pliers to bend the wire to form a 'D' loop. Cut to length with snips. File the tip of the pin to a gentle point which protrudes just beyond the end of the catch. ◀

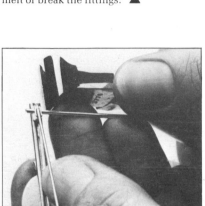

**7** Thread the loop end of the pin into the hinge and then thread a piece of hard silver wire through the same hole. The wire should fit firmly, so that, when you snip the end off, the wire does not fall out. ▲

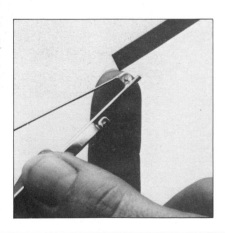

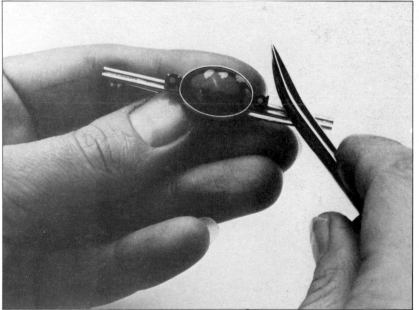

**8** File the wire flat. Tap the wire on a steel block with a riveting hammer until it splays out on either side of the hinge you have selected. ◀

**9** Set the stone, using a rubover setting tool or a burnisher. Next set the two little stones. Polish and clean. ▲

# Wire work

Wire, in some form or other, is an integral part of virtually every piece of jewellery – from brooch pins and ear wires to enamelling and fine filigree work. This versatility is partly due to the varied shapes of wire that can be used – flat, round, half-round, triangular, rectangular and square. In addition, wire is readily shaped into ovals, scallops, tears and stars by using a draw plate (see below). Alternatively, wire can be twisted, plaited, forged and coiled into a multitude of shapes and patterns.

Wire can be obtained in a wide range of sizes, or gauges; varying from very fine wire, known as spool wire, to thicker wire which resembles metal rod. I have used metric measurements, but it is useful to know the equivalent gauges (see table on pp.148-153).

It is important to master the basic techniques of wire work before you attempt more ambitious techniques, such as filigree. I suggest that you start by using round wire, as this is the easiest shape on which to practise the basic wire-working techniques; then, as your skills and confidence increase, you can move on to more elaborate shapes and other types of wire.

**Drawing down wire**

Wire can be made thinner, or reshaped, by pulling it through a draw plate. This is a steel plate with rows of holes, gradated in size or varying in shape.

Select a convenient length of wire and file the end to a point. Anneal (see p.45). Fix the draw plate in a secure bench vice; then, using draw tongs, or large serrated pliers, pull the wire through a hole just slightly smaller in diameter than that of the wire itself. You should pull the wire in one swift, sharp movement, being careful not to pull too hard or you may overbalance. As the wire is drawn through the plate, it stretches and becomes thinner. Repeat this process until the wire reaches the

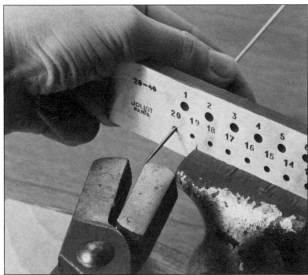

**Wire shapes 1** figure of eight coils; **2** star with mitred joins; **3** plait; **4** spiral coil; **5** twist; **6** simple ring; **7** strips hard-soldered together and curved; **8** crescent with mitred joins.

**Draw plates** A draw plate (above) is used for reducing the width of round wire, while a fancy draw plate (below) changes the shape of the wire.

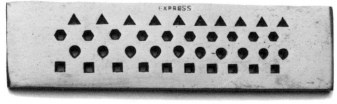

required size, or shape. The wire will have to be re-annealed every so often, otherwise it will become work-hardened and liable to break.

## Twisting and plaiting wire

Twisting wire is one of the simplest wire working techniques; yet it can be used to produce a surprisingly wide range of patterns. You can use twisted wire as the basis of your design, as one of the main elements in the design or purely as decoration.

You need two lengths of copper, or silver, wire. Before you begin the process of twisting, both wires must be absolutely straight. Anneal the wire and fix one end in the bench vice; then, using draw tongs, gently pull the wire straight. When both lengths of wire are straight, secure them firmly in a bench vice. Using parallel pliers, or draw tongs, twist the wire until the strands are tightly bound together. If the wire has been correctly annealed and straightened, the wires will twist evenly, but they may have to be annealed again before the process is completed. Alternatively, hook one length of wire around a nail, which has been firmly embedded in your workbench, and twist the wire as described above.

You will need three lengths of straight wire for plaiting. Anneal and straighten, using the same method as for twisting wire. Fix the ends in the bench vice and plait, pulling the wire tight as you proceed.

## Coiling wire

Coiled wire is an attractive form of decoration. You can make coils of varying sizes or figures of eight. To coil wire, you will need straight, annealed wire, as before. Firmly gripping one end of the wire with round-nosed pliers, bend the wire around the tips of the pliers until you have formed a small central coil. Hold this central coil together with parallel pliers and continue the coil, using a twisting movement. As long as the wire is soft it will coil smoothly, but as soon as the wire becomes work-hardened you will have to anneal it again. To secure the coil, run solder along the joins.

## Making a wire join

A multitude of designs and shapes can be made by using angled wire to form mitred joins. Make sure that the piece of wire you are using is straight (see above) and then cut it into suitable lengths. Hold each piece of wire firmly to prevent it from turning and file the tips until they form an acute angle of about 20 degrees. The two filed tips must mate exactly, so your filing should be steady and accurate. Solder the two pieces of wire together so that they form a 'V' shape. This is your basic shape and, by adjusting the angles, it can be used to make shapes as varied as a star or a crescent moon.

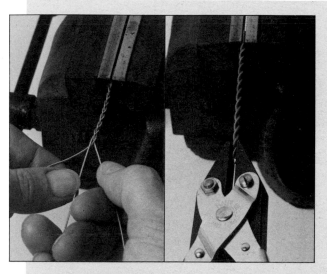

Plaiting wire (left) and twisting wire (right).

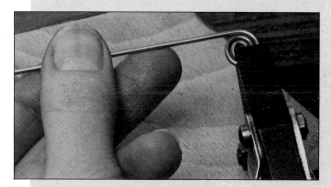

Coiling wire, using round nosed pliers and then parallel pliers.

Filing wire at an angle to form a mitred join.

# Filigree earrings and brooch/1

Filigree, though fiddly to execute, is often so attractive that the effort it takes is well worthwhile. You solder tiny pieces of wire together to form the patterns and shapes you require.

As well as sufficient 0.7mm silver wire for the filigree shapes themselves, you will need two drops and two matching beads. You will also need to buy two silver ear posts and some butterfly screws. These should be flat based. For the brooch, you will need square silver wire about 3.5cm long and 2mm thick, brooch fittings and a pin, plus a setting for the stone. Here I have used a 3mm-diameter garnet and a six claw setting.

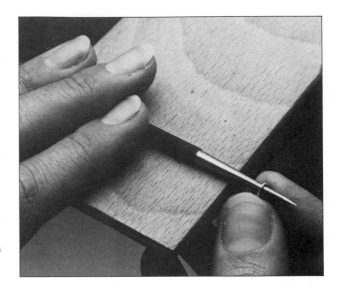

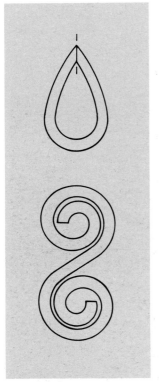

**1** **Making filigree earrings**
Use a scriber as a pattern for twelve teardrops, which you make from 0.7mm wire. File the ends, so that they can be soldered into a point. Make twelve in all. ▶

**3** Now solder the shapes to create the pattern. This is tricky and delicate work and you will need lots of very small pieces of hard silver solder for it. All the shapes must be flat to enable the joins to be soldered successfully. Take care not to use too much solder as this might clog the design. ▲

**2** Use eight annealed (see p.45) lengths of silver wire, each about 1cm long, for the spirals that make up the outer part of the earrings. Bend the wire around roundnosed pliers carefully, making sure there is the same number of coils at either end. Hammer flat on a steel block. ▶

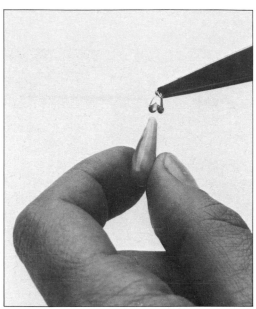

**4** Glue the silver cap to the coral drop with an epoxy glue. You can buy the cap or make your own. ◀

**5** Use a piece of straight nickel wire about 2.5mm thick for the jump rings. Secure the nickel wire in a vice and wrap annealed *(see p.45)* silver wire around it tightly to make the rings. Make this easier by securing one end of the silver wire as well. ▼

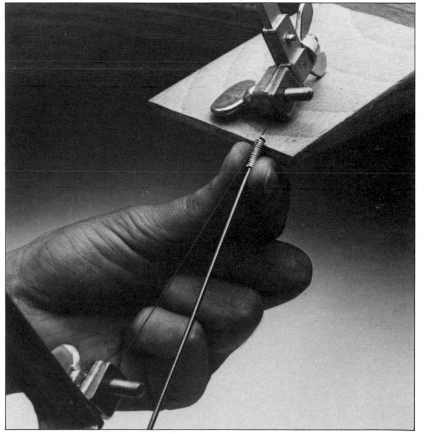

**6** With the nickel wire still in position, cut neatly straight down through the middle with a fine blade. Hold your work securely with your fingers. ▶

# Filigree earrings and brooch/2

**7** You need two lengths of 2.5-3cm silver wire for the top of the earring. Make the spiral coils in exactly the same way as you made the double-ended coils earlier, the difference being that you now make one continuous coil with a loop at the bottom to take the drop (below). Make sure that the wire is well annealed (see p.45) before you start and that the coil is flat when you finish. Run hard silver solder round the spiral and pickle (see p.45). Solder the stud to the back with hard solder. Pickle.

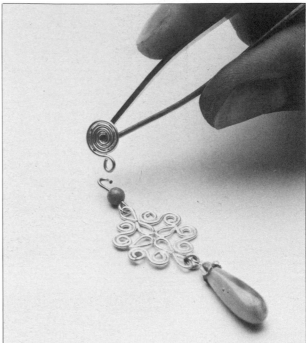

**8** Thread the coral bead on a length of silver wire with a loop at each end. Assemble the earring, using two jump rings to suspend the drop. Clean up the filigree work with emery paper and polish. ▲

**1** **Making the brooch** Use the square silver wire for the brooch's base. File off the ends and emery smooth. Then make two spirals and a coil as you did before, making sure all the pieces are flat by hammering on a steel block. ▶

**2** Solder the setting into place, using hard silver solder. Here, I have used a claw setting, which holds a faceted stone; you can use a cabochon if you prefer. ▲

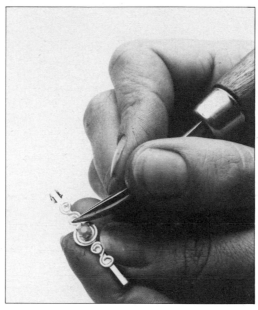

**3** Find the centre of the base. Position the central coil and flank this with the two spirals. Solder in place, using tiny pieces of solder and heating gently and carefully until the solder just runs. Then, using hard solder, fix the brooch fittings to the rear of the piece, supporting the delicate filigree with cotter pins. Pickle and wash. ▲

**4** Set your stone into the mount with a burnisher and fix the pin to the back (see p.76). Polish. ◄

The finished pieces show what can be achieved. Before starting work on the actual project, try out patterns using cheap copper wire, as this will help you to get used to the techniques.

# Working with plastics/1

The plastics most commonly used in jewellery making are perspex, acrylic resin and epoxy resin. Perspex is a plastic that comes in solid form – either in sheet, rod or tube. Acrylic and epoxy resins come in liquid form and are converted into solids by the addition of hardening agents.

## Resins

Acrylic and epoxy resins will solidify when combined with a hardener. This chemical reaction is known as a 'curing process'. Because there are various types of resin and hardener, and because the hardeners react in different ways, it is essential to select the correct combination. Resins can be bought from craft stores or sculpture supply stores. The shop assistants should be able to give you information about selecting resins and hardeners and instructions on how to use them. Resins come in a limited range of basic tones and can be used in their natural colours. Alternatively, resins can be mixed with a variety of colours, but it is important to choose between those with translucent bases and those with opaque bases. I prefer to use the translucent bases, as I find that the colours are clearer and brighter than the opaque bases.

Provided you keep all the safety procedures in mind, working with resins is basically very simple. Pour resin into a disposable container. Add a small amount of colour. Carefully stir hardener into the mixture. The amount you will need will vary, depending on the quality of the resin, but it will usually be between five to ten drops. Let it stand for a few minutes before pouring the mixture into your mould or shape. If you are filling a tiny area of openwork or filigree with resin, then use a syringe. Once the resin has hardened, it should be sanded with various grades of wet and dry emery paper and then polished with aluminium oxide, or with special perspex polishes.

## Resin enamelling

Resins are often set in gold, silver, copper or brass as a substitute for traditional enamels. They can be used to make plique-à-jour – setting translucent colour between openwork metal or filigree – or cloisonné – pouring resin into enclosed areas to make up a pattern or picture. Resins can also be used to repair cracked, or badly damaged enamel, providing you obtain a good colour match.

Resins are superior to enamel in terms of efficiency, speed and price, but they can never surpass the beautiful colours of enamels. The difference between them is like comparing polyester with silk.

## Embedding and marbling

You can create interesting designs by embedding objects – such as shell, wood, arrangments of wire or different types of metal dust – into resin. Position your chosen form of decoration in the mould, or enclosed area, and pour the resin over it. Once the resin has set, sand the surface with emery paper until the decoration is flush with the surface.

A marbled finish of swirling colours can be formed by adding several different colours to the resin and then not mixing them in properly before you pour the resin into the mould.

## Making moulds

If you are pouring resin on to a flat design which has no containing walls or solid back, then great care must be taken to prevent the resin from seeping uncontrollably over areas which are meant to be resin-free. The best way of controlling the resin is to build a surrounding wall from plasticene. Once the resin has set, the plasticene can be pulled away and any residial bits can be cleaned off.

---

### SAFETY PRECAUTIONS

**1.** Do not smoke, as plastics are highly inflammable.

**2.** Do not leave food in your work area, as it could be contaminated with filing dust, or with resins on your hands.

**3.** If any chemicals get into your eyes, flush them immediately with running water for at least ten minutes and then go to a doctor.

**4.** There must be adequate ventilation in your work area, as the fumes are toxic and can cause headaches or drowsiness.

**5.** It is advisable to wear a mask when doing a lot of filing.

**6.** Keep all resins in the refrigerator, or in a cool area.

**7.** It is important never to get resin in your mouth. Therefore, it is sensible to wear gloves or to use hand cream and wash your hands frequently.

**8.** Mix the solution in disposable containers, such as yoghurt pots or old tins, and stir it with a stick or with a disposable spoon.

To create three-dimensional shapes in resin, you will need to make some kind of mould. Moulds can be made from a natural shape, such as a large open shell, or from clay, plasticene, rubber, plaster of Paris, wax or soapstone.

One of the easiest ways to make a mould is to press a solid object, such as a shell or a seed, into plasticene, or into clay, until a clear imprint of its shape has been formed.

Dental wax, used in casting (see pp.66-7), can be carved into a mould. Hollow out a block of wax with scooping rods which have been heated slightly on a candle flame, or on a bunsen burner. Lightly spray the mould with a releasing agent and then pour the resin into the mould.

Rubber moulds can be made for shapes that you plan to re-use (for method see pp.66-7). Rubber silicone can be bought from toy-modelling stores or from craft stores.

### Perspex
Perspex can be bought in rod, sheet or tube form and in a variety of colours, ranging from clear through to black. It can be sawed, bent, engraved, etched, painted or combined with metal. Perspex is a light material, so it can be used to make fairly large pieces of jewellery. Perspex sheets are usually sold with a protective paper sheet, which I always keep as I find them extremely useful for marking out designs.

A jeweller's saw can be used to cut perspex, provided you use coarse blades. Alternatively, you can use a bandsaw, if you have access to one. It is advisable to wear a mask as protection against the thick white dust which is created as you saw perspex. Smooth the rough edges with an old file – the dust will clog up good files – and then finish by sanding them with emery paper.

Perspex has to be heated before it can be bent into shape. This can be done in an ordinary oven using a metal baking tray. It is best to use aluminium trays as they conduct heat very quickly. Take care to keep cooking trays separate from those used for bending perspex. It is advisable to wear gloves when bending perspex and to practise on small pieces until you are able to judge the correct degree of pliability. Heat the perspex at a temperature of 350°F for approximately ten minutes, until it is soft enough to bend. It will reharden after approximately one minute so, if necessary, bending can be done in stages, much like annealing metal.

Perspex is bonded with a special persex glue. To make a transparent join, the edges must be sanded with emery paper until all traces of cloudiness have been removed. Perspex can be engraved by using wood engraving tools and drilled using jeweller's equipment.

**Ammonite earrings from 'Detail'**
These unusual metallic earrings have been made by pouring resin, mixed with copper filings, into moulds made from coil shaped fossil shells, known as ammonites.

Before actually making a piece, it is a good idea to test your pattern on a small piece of resin. Here I have used brass filings and pieces of mesh to make three very different designs.

# Working with plastics/2

**Necklace by Pepe Taylor**
These faceted resin beads were made
by pouring acrylic resin into a rubber
mould and then setting a moonstone
into each bead. Geometric moulds are
timeconsuming to make and the cast
resin shapes will require cleaning and
polishing. The box catch has been
cleverly concealed inside two half
beads.

**Cufflinks and pins by Jackie Cowper**
These pieces are simple and yet very striking. Jackie Cowper has set coloured resins into silver, creating an enamelled effect.

**Perspex bangles from 'Detail'**
Bangles made from clear perspex — one has been left undecorated, the other has been coloured with acrylic paint.

# Acrylic earrings

I have chosen ivory coloured resin for these silver and acrylic resin earrings, but you can vary this by changing the colour of the resin, or by setting shell or metal fragments into the liquid resin and filing smooth.

You will need a sheet of silver approximately 0.5mm thick and about 4.5 x 18 cm in size. To save money, you can use the silver that would otherwise be discarded when you make the inside of the upper part of the earring, as the metal is quite expensive.

**1 Making acrylic earrings**
Pierce out two base shapes and two upper frames to hold the resin. I have used a tear-shaped base and a fish as the central decorative piece, but you could set shell or pieces of wire into the frame as an alternative. ▶

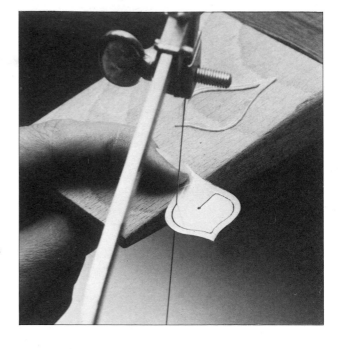

**2** File all the edges. Make sure that the separate pieces are perfectly flat by annealing *(see p.45)* and tapping flat with a mallet on a steel block. ▲

**3** Place the frame over the base, so that the outside edges align, and position the fish in the centre. Flux, and place small pieces of solder around the perimeter. It is better to use too much solder rather than too little, as the excess can always be filed away. Solder, making sure that the solder is confined to the outside of the piece as it runs. Pickle *(see p.45)* and wash in clean, soapy water. ▶

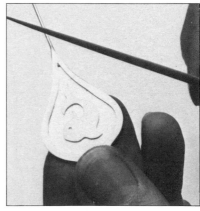

**4** File the edges and then fix a wire to the top of the shape with a softer silver solder. This wire is to be bent around to form the ear fitting, so the join must be well soldered. Pickle and wash as you did before. ▲

**5** Pour about four tablespoons of resin into a disposable container. Add approximately half a teaspoon of pigment and about six drops of catalyst or hardener. Stir with a disposable plastic spoon or stick. Allow to stand for a few minutes and pour into the earring. Always use slightly more of the mixture than necessary, as the resin shrinks slightly in drying. Leave on a warm surface to set. This can take up to six hours. Test with fingertip. It must not feel tacky. ▶

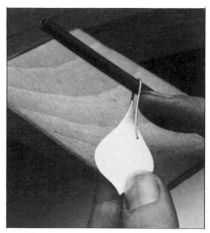

**6** Bend the earwire into a good curve around a piece of rod. File the tip until it is smooth. ▲

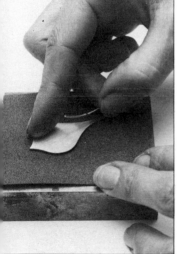

**7** With different grades of wet and dry emery paper, ranging from coarse to fine, smooth down the surface until the resin is flush with the silver. ▲

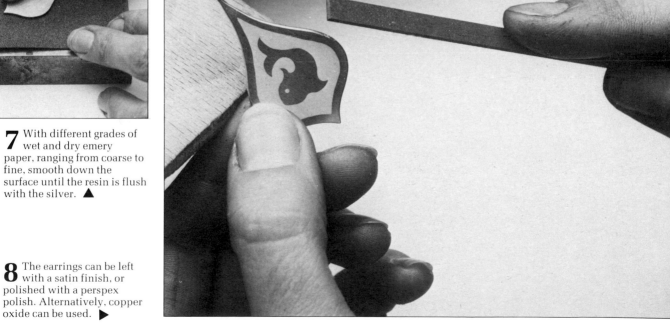

**8** The earrings can be left with a satin finish, or polished with a perspex polish. Alternatively, copper oxide can be used. ▶

# Unorthodox materials/1

If you believe jewellery is made solely from metal, stones and beads, you are making a false assumption and limiting your opportunities. Attractive and original pieces of jewellery can be made from almost any material, including wood, paper, clay, leather, glass and plastic.

**Objets trouvés**

The earliest forms of jewellery were made from objets trouvés, such as shell, vertebrae, feathers and berries. Gradually, as technical skills were developed, objects were drilled, polished and strung together to form necklaces, bracelets and other decorative items. Much of the jewellery made by tribal peoples is still composed largely of such objets trouvés.

Making pieces of jewellery from objets trouvés allows tremendous scope for creativity and originality – it is also great fun. Finding and selecting suitable objects is mostly a question of looking at your surroundings with a new eye. If you use your imagination, all kinds of items, from broken mirror and electrical components to pasta shells and seeds, can be transformed into pieces of jewellery. The list I have compiled is just a beginning; half the enjoyment of making jewellery from objets trouvés is in finding them yourself. Junk shops, jumble sales, flea markets, and hardware stores are all

### OBJETS TROUVÉS

Small door-fittings
Keys
Mouldings used for decorating furniture and picture frames
Curtain fittings – rings, etc
Buttons
Cutlery
Washers
Electrical components
Watch parts
Small ornaments
Fish bones
Animal teeth
Shells
Buckles
Stampings for fire grates
Ventilation covers
Seeds

**'A pair of spectacles' by Tom Binns**
Tom Binns has soldered a brooch fitting to the back of a beautiful pair of old gold-rimmed spectacles and then added a touch of zany humour to the piece.

**'I'm blue for you' by Tom Binns**
To make this unusual medal, Tom has combined a dice, a horseshoe brooch, a picture of Priscilla Presley's eyes, a woven badge (the hand of time) and an antique clock face. The predominant colour of the piece is blue.

potential sources of objects which can be hung, strung or reshaped into necklaces, earrings and brooches. Jewellery designers, such as Tom Binns (see p.15), who specialize in using objets trouvés are inveterate collectors of miscellaneous items, as it is more likely that a particular design combination will be inspired by objects already collected, rather than the other way around.

### Wood
Wood is an excellent medium for jewellery as it can be engraved, carved, inlaid, dyed and decorated, or combined with metals and other materials. You can buy exotic woods from specialist wood stores, or you can re-use wood from second-hand objects.

Gold or silver wire inlay is especially beautiful when combined with ebony or rosewood. Ebony, in particular, lends itself to this technique, as it is a hard wood which is easily carved into beads or other shapes (see pp.112-5). Woods with attractive grains, such as mahogany, olive and rosewood can be carved into beads or bangles and then polished, so that the graining is seen to its best advantage. If you wish to stain, dye or paint wood, it is preferable to choose softer woods with a less interesting grain. There are special wood dyes available but it is also possible to use fabric dyes. French enamel varnish will give dyed wood a bright, clear finish.

You can burn patterns or pictures into wood with a woodburning pencil, or any other burning tool. This technique is known as pyrography and can also be used on leather. If you are using a woodburning pencil, it will come with several tips for producing varied effects. Quick strokes of the pencil will make light lines, while slower strokes form darker and deeper lines.

Marquetry, or inlaid veneer, is another technique that lends itself to jewellery making. Veneer is a thin coating of fine wood which can be bought in rolls or sheets. To make a design in veneer, you will need a mixture of contrasting woods and a sharp knife, or scalpel. Make a template of your design in cardboard, place it on the veneer and cut around the edges. The different pieces of veneer should be cut to fit together – rather like a jigsaw puzzle. Any type of wood can be used as the base for the veneer. Alternately, veneer can be riveted, set or glued to a metal base and combined with ivory or shell.

You can use some of your jewellery tools for sawing or carving wood: a jeweller's saw will cut wood, provided you use a coarse blade; engraving tools will double as wood-carving tools and you can drill openwork designs in wood, by using the same tools and techniques as for piercing metal, although you will not be able to achieve the same intricacy of design.

# Unorthodox materials/2

## Shell

The shells most frequently used in jewellery making are mother-of-pearl, abalone and oyster, but it is also possible to use other types of shell. Shells can be bought from specialist shell stores or from some gem, mineral and craft stores. Sometimes you can buy shell that has already been cut into shapes or carved into beads. Alternatively, you can saw out your own shapes, using a jeweller's saw. However, shell is brittle, so you must cut it with care.

Other natural materials, often used in the past to make jewellery but less readily available today, are tortoiseshell, ivory and horn. The best sources for these materials are flea markets and junk shops.

## Paper

Making jewellery out of paper is both fun and economical. There are three basic techniques – papier mâché, quilling and decoupage.

Making papier mâché involves saturating pieces of paper in paste until it is soft and pliable and then building up shapes in layers. The paper dries to a very hard finish and can be painted, inlaid, varnished, drilled and pierced.

To make your own pulp: soak 25mm squares of newspaper in wallpaper paste, or a paste made from flour and water, and build up your beads in layers. Alternatively, you can use instant mâché pulp, which is available from most craft shops in the form of a grey powder which is then mixed with water. If you are using the commercial pulp, you shape beads by rolling the paste into balls or lozenges and inserting a toothpick, or a piece of wire through the centre to form holes for stringing. You can pull these out once the paper has hardened. You can make bangles by building up layers of pulp around a bottle or a can. Finally, smooth the surface of the papier mâché with emery paper, paint and varnish. In Victorian times, mother-of-pearl was a popular inlay for papier mâché, but pieces of broken mirror or coloured glass make attractive alternatives.

Paper quilling dates back to the Middle Ages when it was as popular a pastime as embroidery or lacemaking. The most traditonal shapes are tight coils, loose spirals, wavy lines and rolled hearts. Cut narrow strips of paper – the length will vary depending on the shape you are making – and roll them around a quill, or a fine knitting needle. Dip each strip in cellulose glue, or wallpaper paste, making sure that the glue completely covers both sides. Press the coils into the required shapes and leave them to dry. When the paper shapes have hardened you can use them as components for necklaces, brooches and bangles. You can also create a filigree or wicker work effect by gluing different types of coil into a design.

Decoupage is an interesting method of decorating wood or papier mâché. Cut out paper designs, or pictures, and glue them to the surface which you are decorating. Coat the design with layers of varnish, rubbing down each layer with emery paper, then buff with wire wool and add a final coating of wax.

## Ceramics

Ceramic jewellery has been popular for thousands of years and is fun to make. You can use self-hardening clay, which can be shaped and embossed and then left to air dry. Alternatively, you might be interested in learning how to model, fire and glaze traditional clay. I suggest starting with clay beads as these are easy to make and allow scope for originality.

## Leather

In the past, leather was used solely for making thongs and straps to carry pendants or talismans; today it is a fashionable medium in its own right. Soft kid leather, snake skin or lizard skin can be stretched over metal bangles and button earrings. Leather can be inlaid into metal (see pp.120-1); embossed, and decorated with a woodburning tool or with metal studs. It can also be decorated with patterns in gold and silver leaf, but this technique requires specialist bookbinding skills.

## Fabrics

There are many ways of incorporating fabric into jewellery making. Silk thread can be used to string pearls or other precious stones. Silk or velvet ribbons make attractive chokers. Silks and brocades can be inlaid into metal (see pp.116-8) and combined with stones. 'Soft' jewellery, made from piping, cords and interesting fabrics and using needlework skills, is an unusual departure from traditional forms of jewellery.

## Glass

The most popular use of glass in jewellery design is in the form of beads, which can be bought separately and then incorporated into your designs. Stained glass makes very effective earrings and is not difficult to make. Basically, you cut coloured glass into the shapes you require for your design, using a glass cutter. Bend strips of copper foil around the edges of the glass and smooth them with a burnisher. Position the pieces of glass so that their edges are touching, brush the copper with baker's fluid and flood the joins with lead solder. Finally, brush the piece clean, using washing up liquid. Broken mirror in different colours can be embedded into clay or resin with unusual results. Andrew Logan's jewellery (see p.28) shows how striking this combination can be.

**Fob by Tom Binns**
This offbeat variation of a fob
is made from a fob chain, a
compass, a miniature globe
and a lightbulb.

**Brooch by Tom Binns**
A protractor, a religious
medallion and a piece of
drawing equipment combine
to form a striking brooch.

# Objets trouvés/1

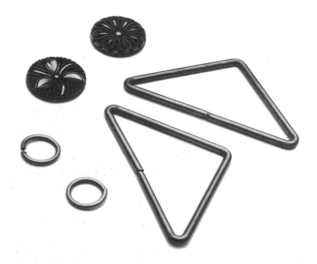

To create exciting costume or theatrical-style jewellery, you can frequently combine all sorts of unusual objects or bits of old jewellery to make an attractive, instantly appealing design. Here, the combination I have used includes a pair of earrings made from two buttons and brass triangular links, the piece being strung together by brass rings. The bangle was made from a metal grating I found in a junk store, while the hat brooch is a combination of feathers, leather, stamped copper and a diamanté shoe clip.

**1 Making the earrings** Snip the backs off the buttons, so that you can glue or rivet clips to them. File the join in the triangular links true and solder together, using easyflow silver solder. Emery smooth. ▶

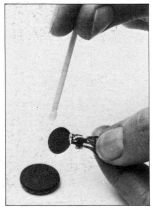

**2** Glue the clip to the back of the buttons with epoxy glue. These particular clips have loops attached from which drops can be hung. ▲

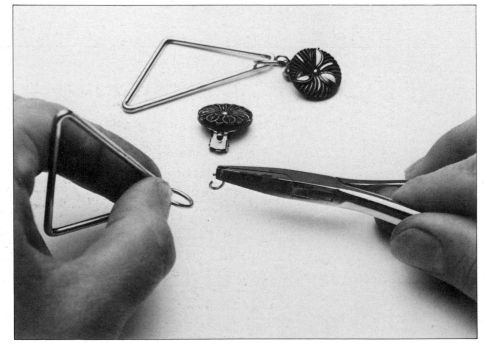

**3** Take the brass rings and attach the triangle to a smaller jump ring, which, in turn, goes through the loop of the clip. Polish. ▶

**1** **Making a brooch** Select an attractive set of feathers to form a plume, using some short and some long feathers. Remove the thick quills. Arrange the feathers on a piece of leather and glue into place. ▲

**2** Cut out a piece of copper – you can use a different base metal if you prefer – designing the shape so that it echoes the shape of the feathers. In this case, I have designed a slightly domed leaf shape. ▶

## MAKING A BANGLE

I have used a piece of nickel grating as my material here – you can buy this at many hardware stores, or you may be able to find some in a junk store. All sorts of different patterns and widths are available and you can easily turn them into exciting items of jewellery.

Cut the strip down to a suitable length of around 15cm, having filed and beaten off the ends to remove any sharp edges that might otherwise dig into the wrist. You should then anneal (see p.45), quench and bend the metal around a bangle stake or mandrel, your aim being to shape a circle with a gap in it large enough for you to slip your wrist through comfortably. Polish.

# Objets trouvés/2

**3** File all edges smooth and lead solder the brooch fittings, keeping them in place with spring tweezers. Remember the solder flows quickly, so just dot it on. ▼

**4** Use nickel rod – this should be around 0.9mm thick – for the pin, bending the hinge end around a pair of roundnosed pliers. File the tip to a gentle point. ▶

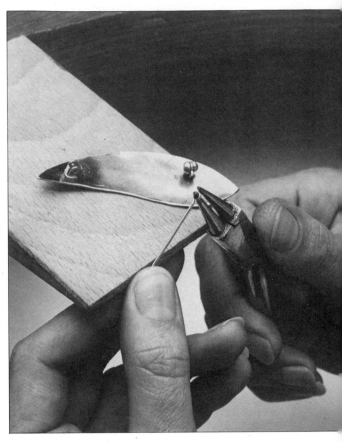

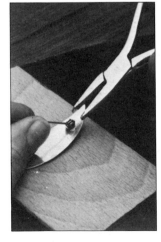

**5** This type of brooch fitting is specifically designed for use with costume jewellery. Put the loop of the pin into the hinge and squeeze together with pliers. ▶

**6** Take the clip off the back of the shoe clip and file off the sharp, rough areas. Solder the diamanté clip to the base of your metal shape. Use lead solder, taking care not to overheat. ▶

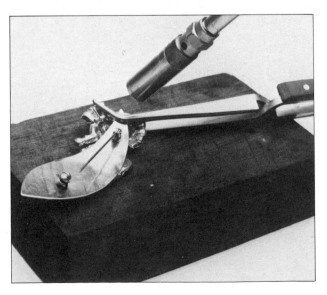

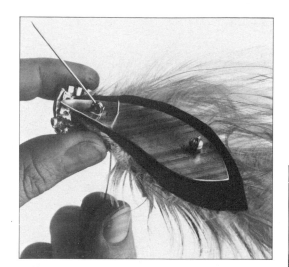

**7** Clean thoroughly and dry. Slot the plume through the gap between the base and the diamanté clip and jam into position. Drill two holes through the clip to the base and thread wire through these to secure the pieces together. ▶

**8** Place your work on a steel block and tap the wires flat with a riveting hammer until the piece is secured. ▲

The examples here clearly show just how easy it is to use unconventional items to make various pieces of jewellery. Use them as a source of inspiration for when you come to make your own designs.

# Advanced jewellery

As with so many skills, the art of jewellery making becomes increasingly complex and intriguing as you learn more and more about it. Now in this section you move on to making pieces of jewellery which not only utilize the basic skills of the earlier sections, but also incorporate more complex materials and techniques.

The specialized techniques described here are skills in their own right. Some will probably interest you more than others and it is worth learning as much as possible about each technique before you invest in any special equipment.

However, as metal is the basis for nearly all jewellery making, it is important to learn the many different ways of decorating it. You can colour, texture and polish the surface; you can engrave, etch and impress patterns. These are just a few of the possible choices. But, a word of warning – before you use any decorative or specialized technique, it is worth experimenting first on a sheet of base metal or else on a piece of work that is not particularly important.

# Specialized techniques/1

Each technique described in this section is a skilled craft in its own right. Therefore, if you are interested in exploring a particular technique in greater detail, I suggest that you buy a specialist book on the subject.

**Engraving**

Engraving is the process of cutting figures, patterns or letters into metal or other hard surfaces, such as stone, glass, bone, plastics and wood.

The tool you will use is called a graver. This steel tool has a cutting tip at one end and a rounded wooden handle with one flat side at the other. There are different tip shapes for producing a variety of cuts.

Hold the handle of the graver in your palm and extend your forefinger along the shaft. The graver is used with the cutting point almost parallel to the metal.

You will need a scriber to transfer the design to the metal, a leather sandbag to support large pieces while you work on them, a clamp for rings, and setter's cement and a block of wood for small pieces. To use the latter, heat the cement so that it melts on to the wood block. Place the article in the soft cement and allow it to cool and solidify. Use methylated spirits to dissolve the cement when you are ready to remove the article. You will also need an oil stone for sharpening the gravers.

Before you begin work on your first article, practise engraving on a sheet of copper. Hold the graver with the handle firmly in your palm. Dig the point into the metal and then carefully lower the handle until the shaft is almost parallel to the surface. Push the graver along gently in 2-3mm sections. It will push out a small curl of metal. Flick the curl aside with the tool, reinsert the point in the metal and continue.

Practise making curves first, and then work on straight lines, which are more difficult. Try the different shapes of graver to see the type of cuts they make. Slip marks that are not too deep can be removed by rubbing along the line with a burnisher, or polished steel rod.

**Working a design**

If the article is to have a polished finish do this before engraving, as polishing can ruin the quality of engraved lines. Next transfer your design to the metal. If you are making a seal, remember that you have to engrave the design in reverse. This technique is known as intaglio. Scribe the design on the metal. Position the article on the appropriate form of support, place the graver on the scribed line and begin cutting as explained above. Cut absolutely on the line, flicking out the metal curl every 2-3mm. Turn the work frequently so that you are always cutting in the same direction. You will find it easiest to cut curves in an anticlockwise direction if you are right-handed and in a clockwise direction if you are left-handed.

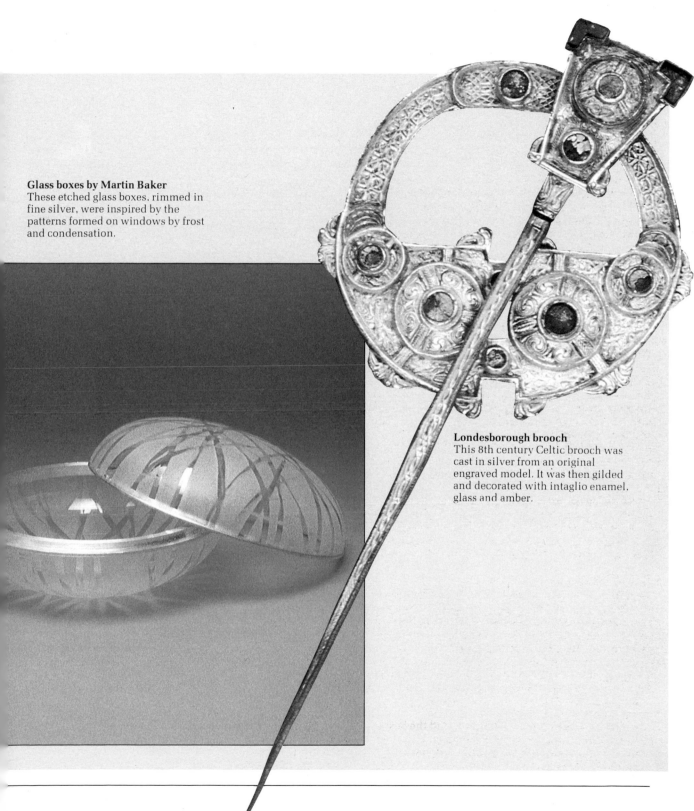

**Glass boxes by Martin Baker**
These etched glass boxes. rimmed in
fine silver, were inspired by the
patterns formed on windows by frost
and condensation.

**Londesborough brooch**
This 8th century Celtic brooch was
cast in silver from an original
engraved model. It was then gilded
and decorated with intaglio enamel.
glass and amber.

# Specialized techniques/2

**Inlaying**

Inlaying is the technique of embedding one material flush into the surface of another. There are many different ways to inlay, including piercing, drilling, carving and etching, and many materials can be used. Fine gold, carat gold, fine silver, sterling silver, copper, brass, bronze, iron and steel can be used in any combination. You can create beautiful patterns using two or three metals of different colour, or by oxidizing silver or gold. You can also grind inlaying materials to a powder, mix them with an epoxy glue, and inlay them. Ebony and other decorative woods, shell, metal dust and acrylic resin can be used in this way. It works best on flat surfaces, but with experience you can also use it to inlay curved and domed surfaces.

You will need chisels and gravers to engrave, carve, chip, gouge, bevel and cut into the metal surface to prepare it for the inlay. The gravers are similar to those used for engraving (see above), with mushroom shaped wooden handles and different shaped tips.

The main types of chisel you will need for inlaying are listed below:
1. V-shaped: for cutting v-shaped grooves, and usually used for making the first incisions.
2. Flat or chipping: for general purposes, chipping, and cutting into thick sheet metal. Hold the tool about 12mm from the striking end; it will remove the metal in curls or chips.
3. Diamond-shaped: for cutting square corners.
4. Cross cut or cape: the tip is narrow with straight edges for cutting grooves and slots.
5. Half-round: for cutting curved grooves and shapes.
6. Round: for making round-bottomed incisions.

You will need punches, which are used to smooth incisions made with a chisel and to push inlay down into its grooves. Like the other tools, punches have different shaped tips for different purposes. A round punch, for example, may be used to make round impressions for the inlay of round wire.

Use a hammer, mallet, or metal rod for striking the punches and chisels. Use a planishing hammer to tap wire into, and splay it flush with, a surface.

You may want to use pitch (see below) to hold the work while you inlay it, or you can secure it to a piece of wood with tacks bent over the edges.

**Piercing metal**

Pierced inlay is the simplest technique and the best one for the beginner to use. A pattern is pierced into a piece of sheet metal, which is then soldered to another piece of sheet metal of the same size and shape.

**Cufflinks by Jackie Cowper**
Jackie Cowper has created simple, but effective, designs by setting resin, embedded with chips of mother-of-pearl and abalone shell, in silver.

Scribe a pattern on to the metal and then pierce it out. Flux (see p.45) the back of the sheet with borax. Place paillons of solder over the area at about 4mm intervals, starting at the edges and working towards the centre. Heat the metal with a blow torch until the solder begins to melt, but do not let it flow yet. Flux the other piece of metal and fix it to the soldered piece with wire. Heat the metal until the solder flows, making sure there are no gaps around the edges. Fill the cells with your chosen inlay. File the surfaces with a flat all-purpose file and then smooth them with emery paper until they are flush with the metal edges. Use an old file on wood or resin.

**Rings by Annabelle Ely**
The striking patterns of these rings have been formed by inlaying gold and silver into an oxidized silver surface.

### Incising metal

Scribe the design into the surface of the metal. Place the metal into the pitch, or secure it to a wood board with tacks bent over the edge to hold it steady. Make the first incision with the v-shaped chisel. Holding the point of the chisel facing you, slant the tool at an angle of about 40° and tap it lightly with a hammer while moving it towards you. Then deepen, broaden, bevel or round the incisions using the appropriate chisels or punches until you have obtained the desired shape or depth of cut. Liquid inlay, such as resin, or metal dust mixed with epoxy glue are best with incised designs.

### Drilling

To make a simple, and very effective, dotted inlay, drill holes into, but not through, the metal in a grid, circular, or spiral pattern. Use wire the same gauge as the drill to inlay the holes. File and then smooth with emery paper until the wires are flush with the surface.

### Inlaying

Cut the material to be inlaid to the shape and size of the incision. Always anneal any metal to be inlaid so that it will spread easily into the incisions when tapped. Push the inlay into the incisions and tap it gently but firmly

# Specialized techniques/3

in place. Using emery paper, smooth the inlay flush with the metal surface.

If you inlay wires, fit them snugly into the incisions, tap them gently into place, solder them in position, and file them flush.

Stone, plastics, wood, ivory, shell and bone can all be inlaid into metal and into each other. Preparing these materials for inlay is similar to incising metal, but each material has different properties and you should always practise carving a new material before embarking on a project. Materials such as stone will be slow and hard to carve, whereas wood will be comparatively fast and soft. However, wood can splinter or crack if it is put under too much pressure or struck too hard. Some materials will expand and others will contract in different conditions. As a precaution, you can secure the inlay with glue. The inlay must always be a tight fit, without ugly gaps between it and the base material. If tiny gaps do occur, you can fill them with epoxy glue, mixed with colour or powdered wood.

## Chasing and repoussé
Chasing and repoussé are the oldest of all the techniques used by jewellers to emboss metal. In chasing, the design is punched into the metal from the front, while in repoussé it is punched into the metal from the back. Confusingly, these techniques are often referred to together under the generic umbrella of 'chasing' – this is because there is a tendancy to use them in conjunction.

To carry out either type of work, you will need chasing and repoussé punches. These are basically the same tools, though the former are flatter and more finely edged than the correspondingly blunter, more rounded-headed repoussé versions. In both cases, the four types are:
1. Bossers, with curved blunted ends for raising the main bulk of the design.
2. Tracers for detailing.
3. Burnishers for smoothing.
4. Texturing tools for producing grained or matt surfaces.
The punches are usually about 12cm long and 6mm square, tapering at the end so that you can see the design as you work on it. You will also need a chasing hammer, which is a light tool, weighing about 115g, with a broad flat head, and a bulbous handle that helps to produce a springing movement when you tap the metal.

During chasing, the metal should rest on a material which will hold it in position and be flexible enough to allow the shaping to take place. The best material for this purpose is pitch, which can be bought, together with a pitch bowl. This heavy cast-iron bowl sits on a leather ring that holds it secure at any angle. To make the pitch malleable, mix two parts of pitch with one part of plaster of Paris. A block of wood, coated with a thick layer of pitch mixture can be used instead of a pitch bowl, but it lacks the manoeuvrability of the bowl.

Draw the design on tracing paper and scribe it on to the metal with a tracer. Anneal the metal (see p.45). Using a blow torch, heat the surface of the pitch gently. Take care not to overheat the pitch, as this will cause it to bubble, so stopping the metal from adhering securely to it. Wet your fingers and then place the metal firmly into the pitch. Allow the pitch to cool. Remember always to wet your fingers before touching hot pitch, or it might stick to your skin. If this should happen, allow the pitch to harden before trying to peel it off.

Hold the punch upright – in your left hand if you are right-handed, or your right hand if you are left-handed – with the 'heel', or working end, touching the design. Tap the punch with the hammer to produce an indentation. Move the punch gently as you tap it, using a light bouncing movement, so that the indentations are not too pronounced. Continue working over the metal in this way until you have completed the design.

As the metal gives and stretches it will harden and will need to be annealed again. To remove the metal from the pitch, heat the metal until the pitch softens and lift it out with metal tweezers. Burn off any pitch left on the metal. Anneal the metal, re-soften the pitch, replace the metal on the pitch and continue working. For intricate patterns, or for work where your design specifies a very high relief, you may have to remove, re-anneal and replace the metal several times.

## Enamelling
Enamel is a form of glass that fuses to metal under heat. It can be transparent or opaque, and is available in a very wide variety of colours and tones. Enamelling is a highly skilled craft and you should be prepared to spend time practising the various techniques.

You will also have to be prepared to buy an enamel kiln, which is an expensive piece of equipment. They are available in various sizes and qualities, heated by gas or electricity. The size you need depends on the amount of work you plan to do. Ideally you should have a kiln with a pyrometer, which measures the temperature inside the chamber. However, if your kiln is not fitted with this instrument, you can buy pyrometer cones – these are used in pottery kilns – which bend and melt at specific temperatures.

You can buy enamel as a powder or in crystallized lumps. I prefer to use opaque colours for fine, or delicate work, as I feel that the transparent colours, being more brilliant, are perhaps a little coarse. You should always prepare enough enamel for use before

**Lapel brooch by
George Fouquet**
This beautiful Art Nouveau
brooch in gold and enamel is
a fine example of champlevé
work.

# Specialized techniques/4

beginning the enamelling process. It is better to make too much rather than too little.

Gold, silver and copper are the metals most suitable for enamelling. Gilding metal and brass present special difficulties and are used only by experienced jewellers. It is best to begin by working with copper to test colours, to get used to the properties of enamel, and to practise the techniques.

Metal and enamel contract at different rates while cooling, which can cause the metal to distort or the enamel to crack. The thinner the metal, the more liable it is to distortion. The shape of the metal may also affect its tendency to distort: flat pieces are more inclined to distort than curved or domed ones.

Enamel fuses at approximately 850°C. This is above the melting point of ordinary solder, so you need to use a special enamelling solder, which has a high melting temperature, on any pieces you wish to join before enamelling. Even then, you will have to be extemely careful during the firing process to prevent the solder from melting in the kiln.

Working with silver also requires special care. It melts at 925°C, allowing only a slim margin between the enamel fusing and the silver melting. As soon as the enamel has darkened and melted, remove the work from the kiln and allow it to cool.

You will need a support on which to lay the metal so that it does not stick to the kiln floor during firing. You can buy stainless steel racks and trivets, or use a piece of steel mesh.

**Enamelling tools**
**1** kiln tray or rack; **2** tweezers; **3** spatula; **4** type of burnisher for pushing the metal surround flush with the enamel; **5** Water of Ayr stone; **6** carborundum stone; **7** shovel; **8** sieve; **9** enamelling support for awkward shapes (used inside kiln).

**Enamelling colours**
Enamelling colours in crystal and powder form. They become paler when ground but, after firing, their brilliance returns. Each colour comes in a variety of shades – there are, for instance, at least ten hues of red, ten of white and ten of green.

# Specialized techniques/5

You will also need a long-handled, two-pronged firing fork to move the support in and out of the kiln, tweezers and a palette knife for handling the metal, and a thick wooden board or metal sheet on which to cool the work after you have removed it from the kiln.

## Preparations

To prepare the enamel lumps, use a pestle and mortar to grind them down to the size of breadcrumbs. They can now be treated in the same way as enamel powder. Add water to the mortar and grind the powder to a very fine dust. The grinding causes impurities in the enamel to rise to the surface. Pour off the cloudy water very carefully, keeping the powder in the mortar. Add clean water, swish it gently, let the powder settle and carefully pour off the water again. Repeat this rinsing process until the water is clear. The enamel must be clean to produce a smooth, even colour. Next, put the enamel on a clean saucer, cover it to keep it clean, and put it on top of the warm kiln to dry. Moisture causes all enamels to deteriorate. If you leave wet enamel to dry slowly by evaporation, it is liable to pit or scum after firing.

To keep spare enamel for further use, wash it to remove any gum, dry it rapidly and immediately store it in an airtight jar. However, it is important to grind fresh powder if you are doing fine work.

You must clean the metal before applying the enamel. Anneal the metal (see p.45) to remove any grease and pickle it (see p.45) to remove any oxide. Be sure to clean off the pickle with a glass brush, while holding the metal with tweezers under running water. Avoid touching the clean metal with your fingers, or you will contaminate it. Use tweezers and a palette knife to manoeuvre the metal.

## Applying enamel

If a large area needs enamelling, coat it with a weak solution of gum tragacanth. Place the metal on a stable support, in the centre of a clean sheet of paper so that its edges are not touching the paper. Sift the dry powder on to the metal through a fine mesh, such as a tea strainer, working from the edges to the centre. When you have covered the metal evenly with a thin layer of powder, tip off any that is loose.

The process used to enamel small areas is known as the wet-laying technique. Moisten the dry powder with distilled water. With a brush or a spatula, lay the enamel evenly on the metal, being very careful not to spill any over the edges. It is important to make sure that the enamel is densely packed and it should never be too thick. Draw off any excess water by very gently touching the edge of the enamel with a piece of clean blotting paper.

## Firing

Gradually bring the kiln up to the required heat and then carefully transfer the metal to a kiln support with a palette knife. Lift the support with the firing fork and place it near the warm kiln to allow the enamel to dry. It is important that the enamel should be dry before it is placed in the kiln, as any moisture left in the enamel would boil during firing and the enamel would lift off.

When the enamel is dry, use the firing fork to lift the metal on the support into the kiln. The duration of firing depends on the size of the kiln, the hardness of the enamel, and the size of the area being enamelled.

Watch the enamel carefully. It will darken and begin to melt. The enamel is fused when the surface becomes pitted like an orange skin. Remove the work from the kiln immediately, and allow it to cool gently on top of the kiln.

The metal oxides that give enamel its colour separate from the glass particles during firing. To remove the oxides hold the work under running water and clean it with a glass brush. Place it near the warm kiln until it is dry, then cover the surface with a second thin layer and re-fire in exactly the same way. Repeat the process once more, but this time do not remove the work from the kiln until the enamel passes the pitted stage and evens out. When the work has cooled it will have a shiny surface, and is referred to as fire-glazed.

## Finishing

Large areas of enamelling may be left with the fire-glazed finish. You can correct an uneven surface by polishing it with a carborundum stone in water. Then clean it with a glass brush under running water, rinse in distilled water and dry. Re-fire the work until it is smooth again. Remove the work from the kiln and allow it to cool slowly.

An opaque glaze can be given a matt finish by polishing it with a Water of Ayr stone and water. Do not re-fire it after polishing as it might discolour.

## Enamelling problems

The most common problem in enamelling is cracking or flaking. This sometimes happens while the enamel is cooling, but it can also take place later. It usually occurs because the enamel is too thick, or else because it has been applied unevenly. However, it may also be caused by traces of pickling acid left in joints and crevices or, if you have used anything other than enamelling solder, by gases produced during firing by metals such as zinc. Additional firings may improve the cracking but, on the other hand, it could get worse.

Discoloration is the next most common problem. Transparent enamels are the most prone to this problem, particularly shades of pink, red and yellow.

## TYPES OF ENAMELLING

**Baisse-taille**
Transparent enamels are fired over a surface in which a
low-relief design has been carved, engraved, stamped or
chased. This technique was perfected by Carl Fabergé
on the enamelled and jewelled Easter eggs he had made
for the Russian imperial family in the late 19th century.

**Champlevé**
Similar to baisse-taille, champlevé work is transparent
or opaque enamel fired over flat depressions carved,
engraved, etched or stamped in the metal, or over
pierced metal soldered on to a base.

**Cloisonné**
In this style of work the enamel is laid within small
enclosures, or *cloisons*, formed by very fine wire, which
is attached to the metal base with clear enamelling flux,
or gum tragacanth.

**Grisaille**
A white enamel design or picture is painted on to a
black enamel background. With each firing some of the
white sinks into the black, gradually creating a tonal
monochromatic effect.

**Limoges**
The technique of painting pictures in enamel was
developed to a fine standard by craftsmen in Limoges in
the 15th century. Many firings are needed to complete a
picture, so the harder colours are painted first, as the
repeated firings would impair the softer colours.

**Pliqué-a-jour**
Transparent enamel is fired in small wire enclosures of
delicate openwork, creating a stained glass window
effect. Gum tragacanth is mixed with the enamel to help
hold it in the open cells, and the work may be placed on
a sheet of mica, to which the enamel will not stick, for
support during firing.

### RECIPES FOR NIELLO

| Ingredients | Pliny | Theophilus | Henrich |
|---|---|---|---|
| Silver | 3 | 2 | 1 |
| Copper | 1 | 1 | 2 |
| Sulphur | 2 | 7-10 | 6 |
| Lead | 0 | ½ | 3 |

## Niello

Niello is a black metal compound of silver, copper, lead
and sulphur, which is used to decorate silver and gold.
Similar to enamelling, niello work employs the
champlevé and cloisonné techniques, and the
compound is fused on to the metal base in a kiln, or
with a blow torch.

You will need at least two crucibles, a charcoal or
porcelain rod, an iron spoon, an oiled steel slab and
quantities of silver, copper, lead and sulphur.

When making niello, always work near an open
window or use an extractor fan, as the fumes from the
lead and sulphur can be noxious.

To make niello, choose a recipe and then measure
out your ingredients as shown in the table. You will
have to experiment to find out which recipe works best
for you.

Place scraps or nuggets of silver in a crucible. Using
tongs, hold the crucible by its spout and heat it with a
blow torch until the metal turns from red hot to a
molten liquid. Add the copper. When the mixture is
molten again, add the lead. Stir the mixture with a
charcoal or porcelain rod, and remove the impurities
with the iron spoon. Keep this mixture molten. Melt the
sulphur powder in a separate crucible. Pour the molten
metal into the melted sulphur and mix thoroughly.
Pour the mixture slowly on to an oiled steel slab, and
allow it to cool and solidify. Using a pestle and mortar,
grind the solid compound into a fine powder.

### Preparing the metal

You can carve or engrave your design into the metal.
Pierce a design in metal and solder it on to a metal base
(see p.47), or solder a pattern of wire straps to the
surface. When the design is on the metal, clean the
metal thoroughly by annealing (see p.45), pickling (see
p.45), and washing it finally in distilled water. Flux the
surface with a weak borax solution. Apply the niello
powder to the design. Niello reduces in volume during
fusing, so heap the powder high in the recesses, taking
care not to let it spill over the edges.

### Fusing

You can fuse niello at a low temperature in a kiln or by
heating it from underneath with a blow torch. Do not
play the flame across the niello: it will burn and pit the
surface of the surrounding metal. Watch the niello
closely until you see it fuse. Remove it from the heat
immediately; overfiring can corrode the metal. Allow
the work to cool off naturally. File off any excess niello,
using old files because of the niello's lead content.
First, polish with a leather buff and pumice powder and
then with a Water of Ayr stone. Finish off with a soft
rouge mop.

# Abalone shell cufflinks

As these cufflinks show, abalone shell and silver make a very pleasing combination, though you could use mother-of-pearl or oyster shell as alternatives. The shell can be bought in flat pieces, or as a whole. If you decide on the latter, take care to use the flattest part of the shell.

You will also need some 0.8-0.9mm thick silver sheet as a base for the round part of the cufflinks and some 1.5mm thick silver wire for the round wall. The carved component is made from 4mm thick silver sheet, while the chain I have chosen is silver belcher chain. You will need just under 2.5cm of chain for each cufflink. The gap between each link should be about 2cm.

**1** Cut a length of 2.5cm silver wire to fit around the shell. As this will make the frame of the cufflink, it must be a snug fit. Take a piece of 1mm thick silver sheet – this should be big enough for two silver rings to be soldered to it – and solder the rings in place. Use plenty of hard solder.▶

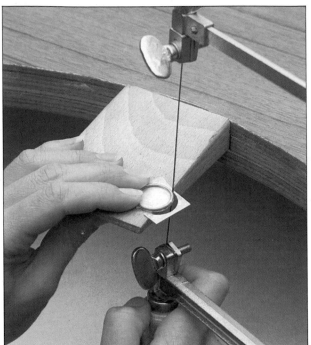

**2** **Making abalone shell cufflinks** Select a flat area of shell. Mark out two circles – the diameter should be about 2cm – and saw them out carefully, using a coarse blade in your jeweller's saw. Work slowly and systematically, as the shell can easily chip. ▲

**3** Mark out the design for the back of the cufflinks on your thick silver sheet. Here, I decided on a petal shape. Cut this out with a very coarse blade (about size 3 or 4). Then file, starting with a coarse file and working up to a fine one. The aim is to literally carve into the silver to turn the petal into a sculpted form, tapering at the points. Take care not to carve away any of the base, as otherwise you will lose the basic petal shape. ▲

**4** Make four loops from 1mm silver wire. Bend short lengths of annealed (*see p.45*) wire around a pair of round-nosed pliers to form the loops. Then upturn and, holding a loop in your pliers, file the ends flat. ▲

**5** Solder the loops to the back of the carved petal shape and the circular shape. Before you start, feed the chain through the loop. This means soldering carefully. Alternatively, use a jump ring to replace the loop. ▲

**6** Pickle (*see p.45*), smooth off any scratches with emery paper, and polish. Bevel the edges of the shell slightly and glue it in place with epoxy glue, or pearl glue. ▲

By comparing the two finishes, you can see that mother-of-pearl is as attractive as abalone shell. ▶

# Ebony earrings/1

Carving ebony is simple and satisfying, as it is a hard and workable wood, while its rich, dark colour makes inlaid precious metals, such as gold or silver, look beautiful. The ebony I used here came from the back of an old hairbrush, but you can buy it in specialist wood stores. Take care not to chip it when you carve.

You will need a 6-8mm thick piece of ebony, plus 1mm and 0.8mm silver wire, which I have arranged in two patterns in the ebony. Use a scriber to score out an egg shape as shown here. Saw around the outside line first, drill, and then saw around the inside one. You are now ready to start inlaying and carving.

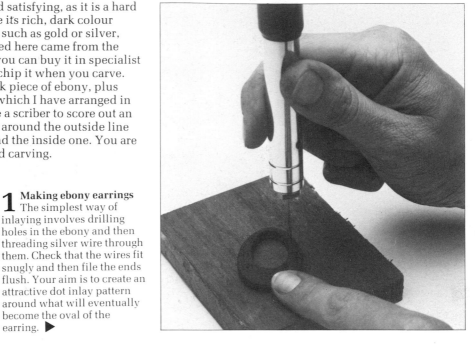

**1 Making ebony earrings**
The simplest way of inlaying involves drilling holes in the ebony and then threading silver wire through them. Check that the wires fit snugly and then file the ends flush. Your aim is to create an attractive dot inlay pattern around what will eventually become the oval of the earring. ▶

**2** I have used two sizes of silver wire – 0.8mm and 1.2mm – to vary the size of the silver dots. You could use more if you want a really elaborate pattern. ▲

**3** Snip off the ends of the wires and file flush with the surface of the ebony. The wires must fit tightly, as otherwise they will fall out. ▶

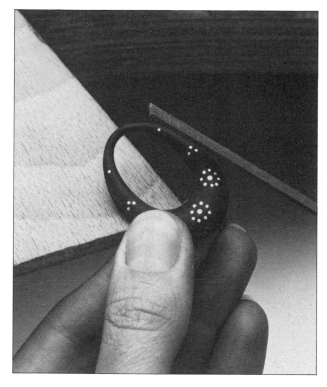

**4** Start carving with an all-purpose file, working gradually around the wood to create a continual curve. Do the same on the inner circle with a half round file. Then, continue carving with an assortment of files, starting with a coarse file and working up to a fine one. Your aim is to make an otherwise flat surface into a smooth, curved sculptural form. Wrap emery paper around your fingers and use it to refine the design. The ebony will gradually smooth and the grain will start to show. The inlay should fit flush with the surface of the wood. Polish on a tripoli wheel. ◀

**5** You use the same type of cabochon setting as you did for the 'cab' earrings (see p.56). Later, you can make an ebony bead to fit in it – a bead about 6mm in diameter is ideal. ▲

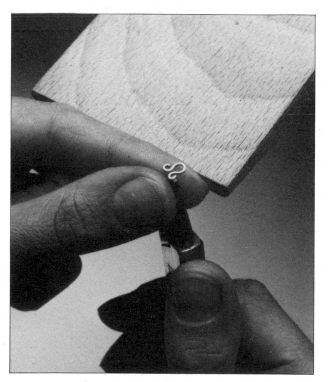

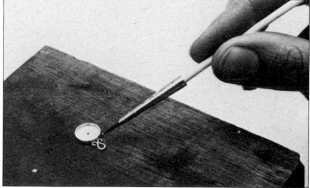

**6** Curve some 1mm wire around a scriber and bend it back with round-nosed pliers to form a fancy loop. Make sure that the wire is well annealed (see p.45); the loop's base should be in the centre of the wire. ◀

**7** Solder the fancy loop to the base of the setting. ▲

# Ebony earrings/2

**8** Make another fancy loop from 1mm silver wire. This will be used to attach the top part of the earring to the egg shape. Here, I have made a fancy 'S' shape with a larger loop at the bottom for the ebony drop. ▲

**9** This fancy shape is used to attach the drop. Secure it with a dab of superglue. ◄

**10** Make the bead by scoring out two circles, each around 6mm in diameter, on the ebony. Carve into a 'cab' shape and smooth. ▼

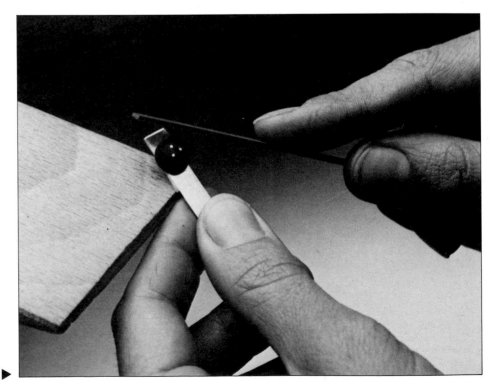

**11** Carving such a small shape can be tricky. Here, I have stuck the material down on to a flat piece of wood with double-sided tape, positioning it to be accessible from all angles. ►

**12** Test the bead for size and put to one side while you solder the stud to the back of the setting, propping up the little fancy loop with cotter pins. Pickle (*see* p.45). ▼

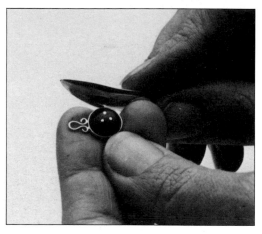

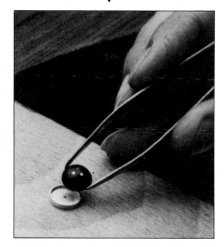

**13** Use a burnisher to set the wooden bead. Take care not to exert more than a very gentle pressure, as wood is comparatively soft when compared to stones. Polish and then attach the drop part of the earring. ◀

**14** If you like, you can wax the finished earrings to get a sheen finish. To show you how easy it is to develop design alternatives, I have left the tops of these earrings plain. ▶

# Metal earrings with fabric inlay/1

By combining fabrics with metal, you can create unusual and eyecatching pieces of jewellery. For these earrings, I have used silk brocade, padded with interfacing for a cushioned effect, set into a metal frame.

You will need 2mm round brass or silver wire, 0.8-1mm thick brass or silver sheet, glue, doublesided tape, card and clip fittings. Start by drawing a template for your basic shield shape, cut it out of the base sheet and score outlines for the edging.

**1 Making inlaid earrings**
Cut lengths of wire for the edging, allowing a little extra for filing and joining. Anneal *(see p.45)* the wire and bend it into a curve around a mug or a cup. Check the curve against your pattern for fit. ▶

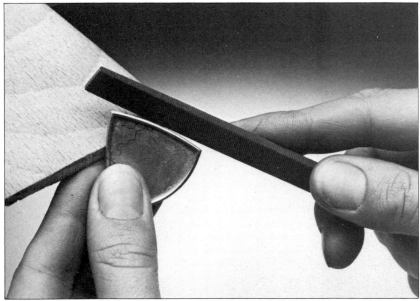

**2** Mark the exact length of wire required with a scorer and file the ends until the three pieces of wire meet at an accurate angle. Silver solder all the joins and then solder the frame to the base, first making sure they are both flat. Saw around the frame and then file until the edges are flush. Smooth the edges with emery paper. ▲

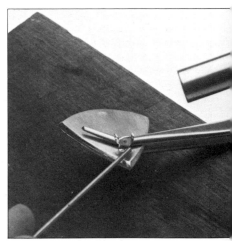

**3** Once the back of the earring is flat and smooth, solder the hinge of the clip to it. Use easyflow solder if you are working in silver, or silver tin solder if you are working with brass. The clip part of the fitting must be added after soldering, as otherwise the heat the process involves destroys the spring mechanism. ▲

**4** Complete all polishing. Make a cardboard base – this should be marginally smaller than the inlaying area to allow for tucking under the edges of the silk. ▼

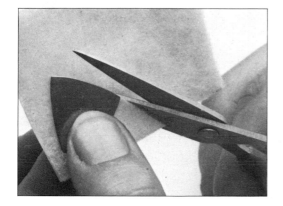

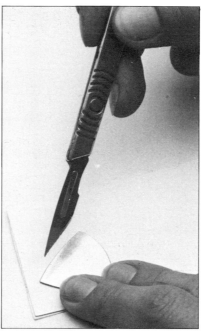

**5** Cut a piece of padding from interfacing or thin foam and stick it to the cardboard base with doublesided tape, or a paper glue. The padding should be smaller than the base by a 3mm margin. ◀

**6** Select a silk or a brocade and fix doublesided tape to the back. Cut out, making sure that you allow sufficient extra material for tucking under the cardboard. Peel off the protective paper. ◀

# Metal earrings with fabric inlay/2

**7** Fix the silk or brocade to the cardboard base, tucking the edges under to prevent fraying. ▲

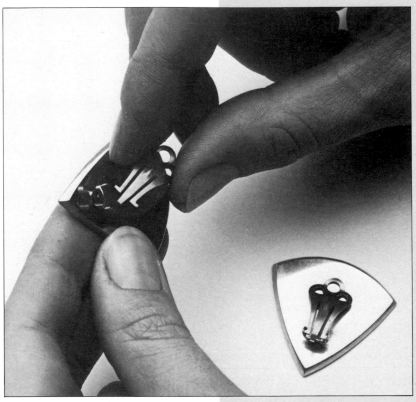

**8** Glue the silk shape into the metal frame, tucking all the edges neatly under the wire with a scriber or a compass point. ▶

**9** Fix the clip to the hinge and secure it in place with all-purpose pliers. Depending on what type of earring clip you have chosen, you may need to rivet it into place. ◀

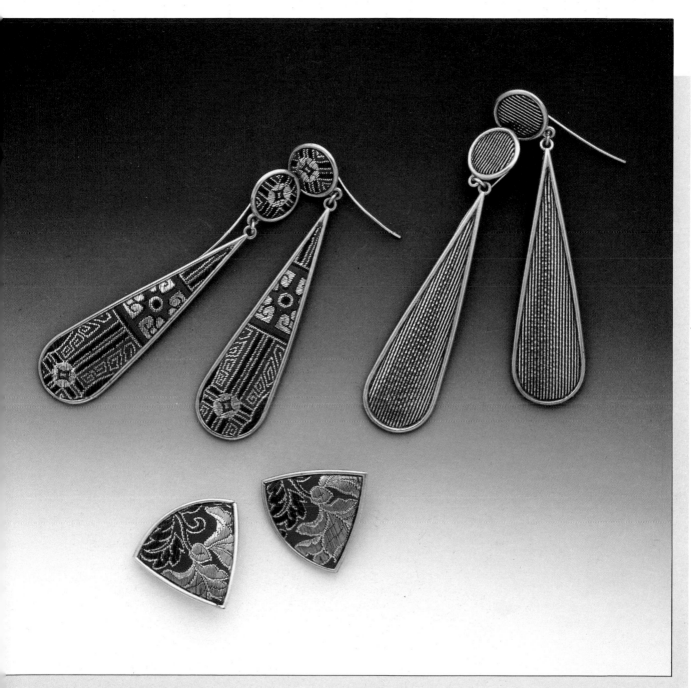

You can make these gold plated drop
earrings in exactly the same way as the
the shield earrings. I have used silk
brocade and silver lamé for the inlay, but
you can choose a different combination.

# Earrings with leather inlay

The basic techniques needed to make these earrings are the same as the ones used to make the earrings with fabric inlay *(see pp.116-9)*. You will need 0.8mm thick sheet and 1.5mm wire in either silver or brass. The triangular edging will need careful filing, as the joins must be true. The top angle of the triangle should be approximately 40°. Solder the wire frame to the sheet with hard silver solder.

**1** **Making earrings with fabric inlay** The backs of the earrings must be filed flat with emery paper before you solder bought, flat-based studs to them. Pickle *(see p45)*. If you decide to have the earrings plated, it must be done at this stage. ▶

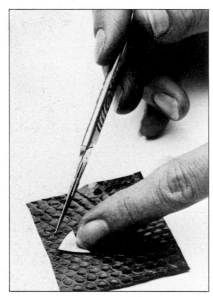

**2** Make a pattern of the inside area of the earring. Stick doublesided tape to the back of the leather and cut out the triangular shapes with a scalpel, allowing enough extra material for tucking the edges under the wire. ▲

**3** Stick the leather inlay in position, tucking the edges under the wire with the point of your scalpel, or with a pin. ▶

These examples show how you can vary the use of leather inlay. They include black leather inlaid into large hoop earrings (*top left*), a bar brooch combining leather and snowflake obsidian (*top right*), leather and black-banded onyx clip earrings (*bottom left*) and the finished triangular earrings, which I have made in gold plated brass, with a red snake skin inlay (*bottom right*).

# Plating, oxidizing and colouring/1

Metal surfaces can be coloured by a variety of methods. Some metals change colour when heated; others respond to electrochemical techniques, such as anodizing, which produces an anodic film on the surface of the metal, thus changing its colour. Brass and copper will react to acid, turning dusty pink or bright turquoise.

Oxidizing causes copper to turn black and silver to turn shades of blue and grey. Electroplating is used to deposit a coating of precious metal on base metals. Striking patterns can be formed by mixing different coloured metals or by using stopouts during the process of electroplating.

### Electroplating

There are several reasons for using electroplating as a finish for pieces of jewellery. The most obvious of these is cost – you can produce a gold or silver finish without the expense of using gold or silver throughout.

Rhodium and platinum plating add extra lustre to white gold. Electoplating can also be used to provide protection against corrosion. Gold, for example, will not tarnish in the same way as copper or silver, which oxidize over a period of time.

Electroplating requires highly specialized equipment and the cyanide salts used in plating baths are deadly poisonous. It is essential, therefore, to take your jewellery to a professional plater.

Although you will not be doing your own plating, it is useful to have some knowledge of the technical process. The plating solution is based on a salt of the metal to be plated – silver cyanide is used for silver plating – and combined with other chemicals which increase the conductivity of the solution. The solution is electrolyzed by passing a direct current through it and the charged particles, or ions, are attracted to the piece of jewellery which is being coated.

Plated coatings are measured in microns, which are

**Anodized tantalum mesh**
Anodizing mesh, rather than sheet metal, produces soft, translucent colours, with a lovely sheen.

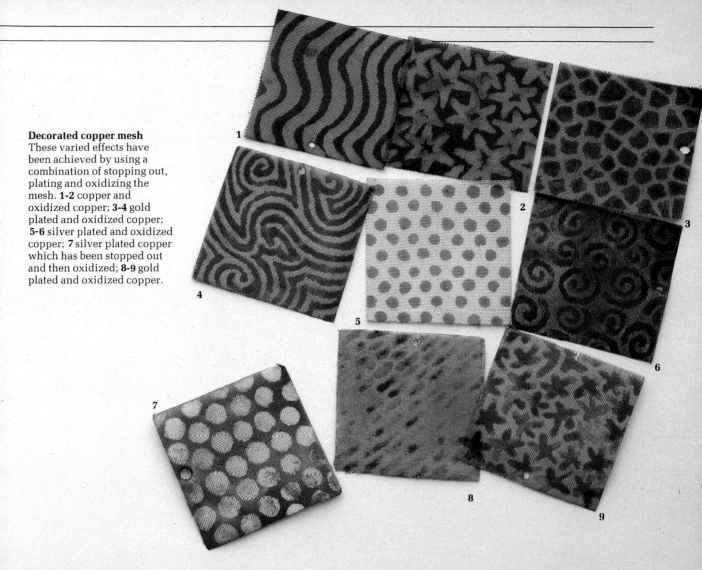

**Decorated copper mesh**
These varied effects have been achieved by using a combination of stopping out, plating and oxidizing the mesh. **1-2** copper and oxidized copper; **3-4** gold plated and oxidized copper; **5-6** silver plated and oxidized copper; **7** silver plated copper which has been stopped out and then oxidized; **8-9** gold plated and oxidized copper.

equivalent to one thousandth of a millimetre. The thickness of the coating depends on the function of the object, or on the quality of the plating. 'Flash' plating – used on most fashion and costume jewellery – covers the base metal with a deposit of precious metal which is less than one micron thick. However, better quality jewellery is plated with a layer of one to two microns, thus giving the piece greater durability and protection against corrosion.

Before you take metal to a plater, it must be absolutely clean. Soak the piece of jewellery in hot water and a strong detergent, use a soft brush to clean all the surfaces and then rinse the piece in cold water. It is important to remember that the plating will reflect the original finish of the piece. A matt finish will remain matt after plating and, if you have not polished the surface sufficiently, the plating will appear dull.

**Types of plating**
There are a wide range of gold alloy colours available, ranging from pure gold through the various shades of red gold, green gold, yellow gold, pink gold and pale gold.

Before any base metal is silver plated, it is often given a preliminary coating of nickel in order to increase the lustre of the coating. Silver plating is also used to re-coat silver which has been blemished by fire stain. Fire stain is unwanted oxidization caused by overheating the silver. In most cases, it is possible to file off the stain, but sometimes silver plating is the only solution.

Palladium is used as an alternative to rhodium when a thicker layer of plating is required, although it is not as hard or as reflective. White gold, plated with either platinum or rhodium, is used in combination with paste, rhinestones, diamonds and aquamarines to enhance the brilliance of the stones. Copper and nickel are generally used for underplating precious metals. This 'undercoating' seals off any pores in the base metal, thus producing a more effective surface for the plating. Underplating also increases the lustre of the precious metal plating.

# Plating, Oxidizing and Colouring/2

## Stopouts

Attractive patterns can be formed by using rubber stopouts during the plating process. The plating adheres to the exposed metal, leaving the unexposed metal its original colour.

The surface of the metal must be absolutely clean before the rubber stopout is applied or it will not adhere properly to the surface. Using a paintbrush, apply the stopout directly on to the metal. When the plating process is complete, remove the stopout with a petrol-based chemical called Xylene.

I suggest you start by using copper mesh to practise this technique, since the rubber adheres easily to its surface. Then, as your confidence increases, you can move on to etched or matt finishes. Highly polished metal is the most difficult finish to stopout, but it is worth practising until you achieve success, as the resulting patterns can be very attractive.

If your design incorporates a pattern which uses more than one metal – silver and gold on copper, for example – you will have to stopout the areas that you want to remain copper and then take the piece to be silver plated. Next, you will have to stopout the copper and silver areas and take the piece to be replated with gold. However, since this means several trips to the platers, it is an expensive and inconvenient method of producing a pattern.

## Oxidization

Oxidization is a natural process, which occurs as metal is exposed to air and moisture over a period of time. However, it can also be induced, by using heat or chemicals, to create a variety of surface coloration.

There are several metals which change colour when heated; copper is the one most commonly used for jewellery making. As copper is heated, the surface forms a scale of cupreous oxide, which is pink initially but changes to red with further heating. As the heat increases, the oxide layer thickens and turns black. To preserve this colouring, allow the copper to cool naturally and then quench the metal in oil. By gently rubbing off the black layer to reveal the underlying red layer, you can create a speckled effect. The oil enhances the colour and fixes it temporarily, but you will then have to apply a final coat of lacquer, or fixative.

## Oxidizing using chemicals

Colouring metal surfaces chemically produces some striking effects, but it is essential to take great care when handling the chemicals. Always keep the safety precautions listed clearly in mind.

You will need some special equipment for working with chemicals: a glass beaker or dish, which is heat-resistant and large enough to avoid any danger of the chemical slopping over the edge; an old paintbrush for stippling; copper or brass wire for dipping objects into the chemical solution; plastic tweezers; electric hotplate or gas ring; thermometer (optional); rubber gloves; mask; fixatives – metal varnish and artist's fixative; lacquer or wax.

## Ammonium sulphide

Ammonium sulphide turns the surface of copper, black or gunmetal grey and colours silver, black, grey, sky-blue or purple. Variations in shading are created by controlling the exposure of the metal to the chemical. You can paint the undiluted chemical directly on to the metal surface with a paintbrush. Alternatively, you can dip the piece of jewellery into a dilute ammonium sulphide solution.

When painting on the ammonium sulphide, first pour a little amount into a small container. Immediately replace the lid, as ammonium sulphide gives off a very unpleasant smell. Using a pair of tweezers, grip the piece of jewellery and gently heat the metal until it is almost too hot to touch, but not hot enough to change colour. Paint the ammonium sulphide on to the metal, using an old paintbrush. On contact with the chemical,

---

### SAFETY PRECAUTIONS

**1.** I recommend strongly that you learn a little about the properties and dangers of the chemicals you plan to use, before you start working with any of them.
**2.** Do not overheat chemicals, as this produces dangerous fumes.
**3.** Chemical contact with skin can cause irritations or burns.
**4.** If any chemicals should get into your eyes, rinse with cold water for at least five minutes and then immediately go to a doctor.
**5.** Always wear protective gloves.
**6.** It is advisable to wear a fume mask.
**7.** Work under a fume extractor, or near an open window.
**8.** Keep chemicals in tightly sealed containers, out of the reach of children and animals.
**9.** Store chemicals in the refrigerator, or in a cool place. Clearly label all containers.
**10.** Take care not to spill chemicals.
**11.** If you dispose of solutions by pouring them down the plughole, make sure that you rinse the sink thoroughly with cold water.
**12.** Always add the chemical solution to water. Never add water to chemicals.
**13.** Dry chemicals should be diluted with a little water so that they dissolve thoroughly when added to the solution.

the metal will turn grey and then blacker as oxidization builds up. You can form patterns by applying stopout before you begin oxidizing. Rinse the piece. By dabbing it dry with a tissue, you will be able to make sure that the colour is even. Although oxidization tends not to wear off, you may wish to fix it with metal varnish or with lacquer.

Surplus oxidization can be removed with a jeweller's cloth. If the piece is engraved or textured, for example, you can emphasize the pattern by removing oxidization from the flat, or raised, surfaces and leaving it in the recesses. If you make a mistake, it is possible to remove most of the oxidization by polishing the surface with tripoli. Alternatively, you can buy a de-oxidizing solution.

If the entire piece is to be oxidized, it best to dip it into an ammonium sulphide solution. It is essential to work in the open air or under an extractor fan, as mixing the chemical with boiling water produces noxious steam. Carefully pour one part ammonium sulphide into a heat-resistant glass dish containing six parts boiling water. Heat the piece of jewellery by placing it in boiling water. Using tweezers, dip the piece into the ammonium sulphide solution. Silver turns brown first, followed by purple, blue, blue-grey, grey and finally black. Controlling this colour shading, takes practice. Dispose of the ammonium sulphide solution immediately you have finished using it. Rinse the jewellery and gently brush the surface with washing up liquid to remove all traces of the chemical.

### Liver of sulphur

Liver of sulphur, or potassium sulphide, produces colour changes ranging from brown through to black, on low carat gold, copper alloys and sterling silver. Liver of sulphur comes in solid form and must be dissolved in warm water. Add 14-28 grams of the sulphur to two parts of hot (not boiling) water. Stir until dissolved and then either paint it on to the piece of warmed jewellery or, if an overall colour is desired, totally immerse the piece in the mixture. The colour will start as a deep yellow and develop through brown to black. Be careful not to overheat the piece, or to apply too much sulphide solution too quickly, as the colouring may form into a brittle film which will peel off. By adding approximately three grams of aqua ammonia to the liver of sulphide solution, you will increase the intensity of the black colouring. Rinse the piece thoroughly.

Hundreds of chemical formulas have been devised to induce pure metals and metal alloys to change colour. Some are more successful than others. I have described some of the basic recipes (see pp.148-53) but, as your confidence increases, you will develop your own methods of producing varying colours.

### Anodizing

Anodizing is an electrochemical process that deposits a controllable coating of oxide on the natural grey surface of certain metals, producing a wide range of bright and subtle colours. The metal most frequently anodized in jewellery making is titanium. It is a light, strong metal that cannot be soldered, so it must be joined by riveting or gluing. As it is not very malleable and does not respond to many of the traditional jewellery making techniques, the most successful use of titanium is in two-dimensional designs.

Other metals suitable for anodizing are aluminium, tantalum, niobium and tungsten. Aluminium can be turned most colours but, although the colours are very definite, the metal tends to reflect through the colour, so that the paleness of the aluminium is always apparent. The more the colour is built up during the anodizing process, the duller the finish will be.

Tantalum, niobium and titanium can be turned a very wide range of beautiful colours — peacock blue, violet, jade green, lime green, magnolia, shades of brown, lilac and yellow ochre. Tantalum and niobium are alloys of titanium, but their colouring is more subtle. Tantalum is the most difficult of the three to obtain, but it produces the finest range of colours. It can be bought in mesh form from industrial companies that make glassfibre. You can use the mesh in the same way as copper mesh (see pp128-131), but it cannot be soldered. After anodizing, the mesh takes on a brilliant shading like that of a butterfly's wings or peacock feathers.

Anodizing equipment can be bought for use in jewellery making, but it is expensive and I would not recommend investing in it, unless you are planning to do a large amount of anodizing. However, there are firms that specialize in anodizing to which you can take your pieces of jewellery for colouring.

If you intend to try your hand at anodizing, you will need a variable voltage power unit, insulated leads and a plastic or glass tank. The equipment and chemicals used for anodizing are dangerous and you should take sensible precautions, including wearing rubber gloves at all times.

Various conducting solutions, or electrolyte, can be used, but the most usual is 10% ammonium sulphate. The piece to be anodized is attached to the anode and immersed in the solution. Changing the voltage produces different colours: the higher the voltage, the thicker the oxide film and the stronger the colours. Aluminium receives a colourless anodized casting, which is dyed and sealed subsequently.

Colour can be painted on to the surface of the metal by wiring a paintbrush to an electric current and then dipping it into the electroconductive solution.

# Plating, oxidizing and colouring/3

However, this process requires considerable technical knowledge and it is inadvisable to try it unless you have complete technical instructions, or you are taught by an experienced worker.

Subtle differences in colour can be obtained by stopping the voltage at a particular number (see chart). For example, a brilliant turquoise occurs around 42-43DC, and cardinal purple around 72-73. However, colour can vary, depending on the machine, so it is advisable to ask the anodizers for a colour chart or to experiment if you are doing your own anodizing.

Titanium can also be coloured by using heat. Very definite pinks, browns and greys can be obtained, using this method, but the colouring process is less easily controllable. A heated needle can be used to draw a pattern on to the surface of the metal or you can obtain an overall colour by heating the item in a kiln.

### Post-colouring finishes on non-anodic metals

After colour has been applied to a metal surface, you simply fix the colour or, alternatively, you can add patterns and highlights. Using engraving tools or a scriber, you can scratch patterns on the surface to expose the base metal colour. The areas to be patterned must be accessible, so the different effects possible will depend on the shape of the object.

You can rub raised surfaces with pumice or tripoli to lift off some, or all, of the colour, leaving the recesses coloured. Alternatively, use a buffing wheel to highlight extruding areas.

Fix colours by spraying them with artist's fixative, or with metal lacquer. You can buy gloss, matt or tinted metal lacquers. The metals must be grease-free before you apply the lacquer or it will not adhere properly. Lacquers dry rapidly and can be applied thinly in several layers.

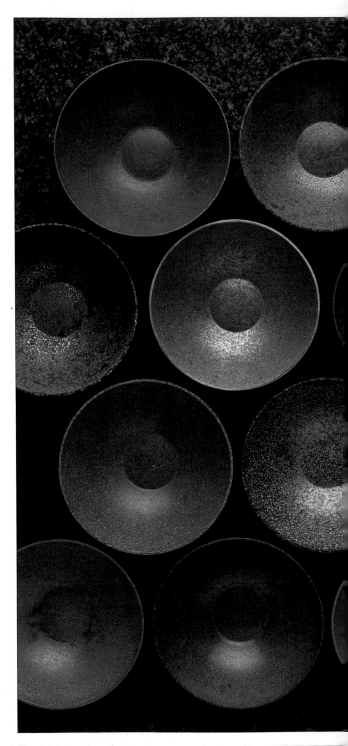

**Sample bowls by Chris Howes**
Chris makes these sample bowls in gilding metal, brass and copper as a means of testing the results of experimental recipes for colouring metals. He spins the bowls on a lathe and then buries them in sawdust, which has been saturated with the chemicals. The fumes from the chemicals colour the metal, while the sawdust gives the surface a slightly pitted finish.

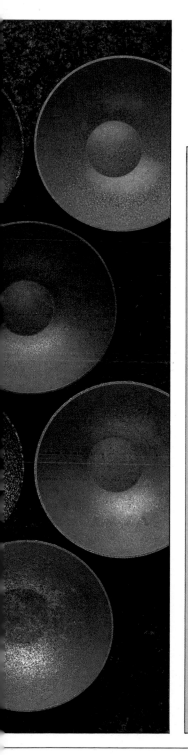

## TITANIUM COLOUR CHART

| Colour | Temperature | | DC voltage |
| --- | --- | --- | --- |
| | Fahrenheit | Centigrade | |
| Pale yellow | 700 | 371 | 3-5 |
| Orange-gold | 725 | 385 | 10 |
| Dark gold-brown | 750 | 398 | 15 |
| Purple | 775 | 412 | 20 |
| Blue-purple | 800 | 426 | 25 |
| Sky-blue | 825 | 440 | 30 |
| Cobalt blue | 850 | 454 | 35 |
| Pale blue | 875 | 468 | 40 |
| Blue-green | 900 | 482 | 45 |
| Green-blue | 925 | 496 | 50 |
| Sea-green | 950 | 510 | 55 |
| Gold-green | 975 | 523 | 60 |
| Gold-green, speckled with purple | 1000 | 537 | 65–70 |
| Rose-gold | 1025 | 551 | 75 |
| Magnolia | 1050 | 565 | 80 |
| Purple gold | 1075 | 579 | 85 |
| Dull purple-blue | 1100 | 593 | 90 |
| Dull green-red | 1125 | 607 | 95 |
| Browny-grey | 1150 | 621 | 100 |
| Mottled grey | 1200 | 635 | 110 |

# Ribbons and bows

M etal is a versatile medium. It can be used even to imitate the quality and patterning of a fabric. These earrings are made from a delicate copper mesh and then gently moulded in a traditional bow shape to create the effect of folded and knotted material.

The metal mesh can be patterned by oxidizing (see pp120-1), which changes the colour of selected areas of the metal. Try experimenting with different patterns. For these earrings I have used a simple spotted pattern, but a tiger-stripe or chequered pattern is also extremely effective against the folds of the metal.

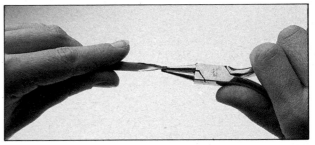

**1** **Making bow earrings** Cut several 6-mm (¼-in) strips from a 0.25-mm (¹⁄₁₀₀-in) thick copper sheet, using a sharp pair of ordinary scissors or metal cutters.

**2** Pinch together one end of each copper strip, using a pair of long-nosed pliers. This will make it easier to draw the strips through a draw plate.

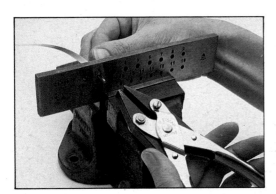

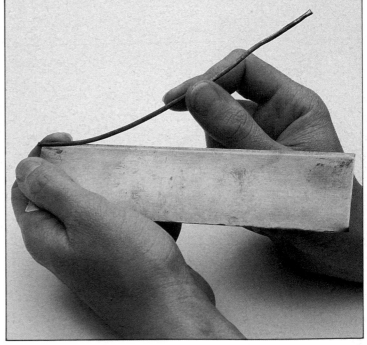

**3** Draw the strips through a draw plate (see p56) until they are almost tubular in shape. Draw the strips first through one of the larger holes to curve them gently, and then through smaller holes in turn until they are completely rounded.

**4** Heat each bent copper strip in turn until the metal has softened and then slide each over the edge of a piece of thin copper sheeting.

**5** Place the copper sheet with the strip attached, on a metal block, and hammer the strip flat.

**6** Cut two templates from copper sheet, one in the shape of a falling end of ribbon, the other in a narrow leaf shape to make the knot of the bow. Mould a length of the copper strip along each side of both templates with a burnisher until each fits snugly in place.

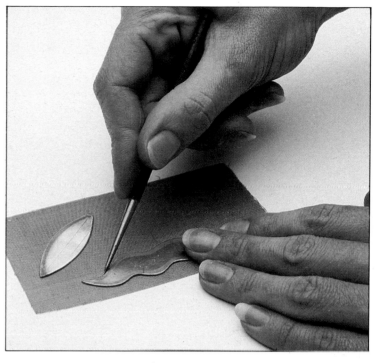

**8** Fit the first strip to the appropriate edge of the mesh shape. Check that it is positioned correctly. Fit the second strip to the other edge, again making sure that it fits snugly in place.

**7** Place a template on a sheet of copper mesh and score around the outline with a pointed tool. Cut around the outline with scissors. Repeat the process with the second template.

# Ribbons and bows/2

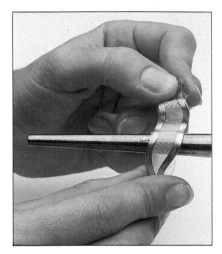

**9** Hammer the edging flat, squashing it down on to the mesh. Anneal (*see p.45*). Cover with sticky tape to hold the shape together and create wave patterns with a ring triblet. Remove the tape, clean and pickle (*see p.45*). ▲

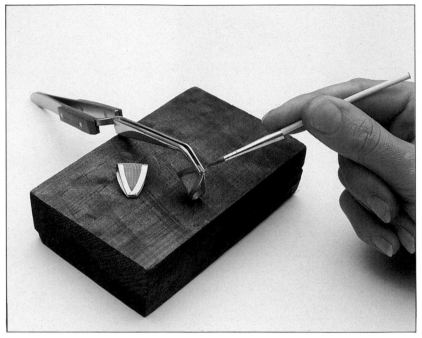

**10** You make the top bow of the earrings as you did the tail, only around the petal-shaped pattern. Bend around a stake to form a loop. Hold the tips together with spring tweezers, solder, pickle and wash. ▲

**11** File the edges of each of the loops with an all-purpose file to get them good and straight. ◀

**12** Supporting two loops with cotter pins, place together and solder with hard solder. Take care not to overheat, as you run the risk of melting the mesh if you do. ▼

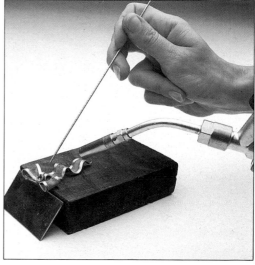

**13** Pickle and boil in soda. Dry. Drill a hole through the centre of the loops of the bow. Solder silver wire to your setting, using hard silver solder. Pickle and thread through the hole. ▲

**14** To assemble the entire earring, use lead solder, applying the solder carefully so as not to flood the mesh. Use cotter pins as supports.

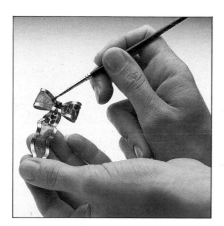

**15** Wash the earrings carefully in soapy water with a little ammonia and then polish. Paint out your pattern with lacquer-mit stopout ready for goldplating. After this, remove the stopout with xylene before oxidizing with ammonium sulphide. ▲

**16** For variety, I set a faceted piece of jet into the earrings. ▶

# Making coloured brass bangles/1

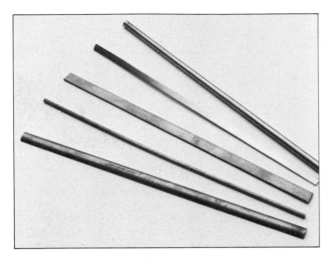

Using the same basic method, you can make an assortment of bangles in varying shapes and colours, using different materials – sheet, tube, wire or rod – of differing thicknesses and sizes. Here, I have chosen 4-6mm round copper rod, strips of copper and brass ranging from 50mm to 1cm in width and 1cm half-round copper rod. All of the heavy copper should be bought in what is termed a 'soft' state – that is, already annealed – so that it will bend easily around a bangle mandrel.

**1** **Making a single bangle** Cut the metal to size - the average length for a bangle is 15-17cm. Anneal *(p.45)*. ◀

**2** Using both hands, bend the annealed metal around the bangle stake and then hammer it into a true curve with a mallet. ▼

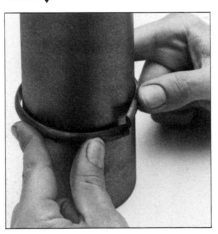

**3** File the ends with an all-purpose file to get a true join. This is important if you are using a thick rod, as otherwise there will be gaps in the solder. Use hard silver solder for thin pieces of metal and easyflow solder on the larger pieces. Pickle *(see p.45)*. ▶

**4** Smooth the solder join with an all-purpose file. ▲

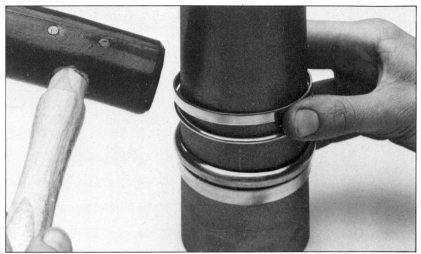

**5** Tap the bangle around the stake again to ensure that you have a good curve. Remove any scratches with emery sticks, starting with a coarse grade and working up to a fine grade. Rub the inside and outside of the bangle with emery paper until it is smooth. Polish and clean. ▲

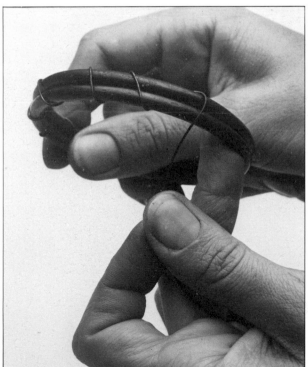

**1** **Making a double bangle** Using the same method as before, make two bangles to the same width. Wrap the two tightly together, using binding wire. ▶

**2** Solder the bangles together with easyflow solder, or silvertin solder, depending on the metal used for the bangles. Clean off excess solder. ▲

# Making coloured brass bangles/2

**3** Make decorative coils from 1.2mm thick copper wire. Anneal *(see p.45)* the wire, grip one end with parallel pliers and bend the wire around them. Keep the shape of the central coil by gripping it firmly with the pliers while you coil. ▶

**5** Emery all surfaces and polish with tripoli. Clean off the tripoli and then set the stones. ▼

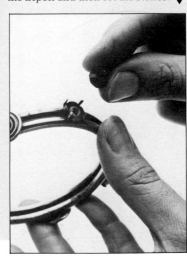

**4** Arrange bought settings and decorative wire coils around the bangle, holding them in place with binding wire. Solder them on to the bangle, using easyflow or lead solder. Clean off any excess solder. ▲

The examples here show how varied
the finishes of your bangles can be.
I have used a mixture of patterning and
colouring techniques — plating with
gold, silver or rhodium; oxidizing;
laquer-mit stop out and amonium
sulphide oxidization; dipping in acetic
acid to form an attractive tarnished
turquoise streak.

# Texturing metal surfaces/1

There are many ways of texturing metal surfaces to achieve finishes ranging from a simple matt polish to complex etched patterns. Your choice of method will depend on the complexity of your basic design, the materials you have used and the type of equipment available to you.

### Texturing using heat

This must be done before you construct your piece, as the heat may destroy any previous soldering. It is inadvisable to attempt this technique on very thin metal as it will probably melt into holes. Heat the sheet of metal with a blow torch until the surface is just beginning to melt. With experience, you will be able to detect the critical point between surface melting and complete collapse; the metal develops an intense shimmer just before it melts completely. Remove the flame at once. The surface ripples – creating a 'lunar crater' texture – as it solidifies. You may have to repeat the process several times to obtain a satisfactory effect. This is a technique which needs practice to perfect. It is almost impossible to control the pattern exactly, but the results can be very striking.

### Hammmering

Using a planishing hammer, or a ball pein hammer, you can create finishes ranging from a light stipple to a dimpled effect. You can also give the metal a bark-like finish with the wedge end of the hammer.

### Glass brush finishing

Polishing metal with a glass brush produces a satin sheen finish. Dip the brush frequently into soapy water during the polishing process and polish until all scratches have been removed. Glass brushes must be handled with care, as the glass threads are apt to break off and could become embedded in your hands.

### Brass brush finishing

Polishing with a brass brush is a quick method of giving dull metal a bright finish. Remove all scratches with emery paper before you start polishing. Dip the brush into soapy water during polishing, otherwise a yellow deposit of brass will accumulate on the surface.

### Fraizers, burrs and buffers

Buffers, which are attached to a wheel or pendant drill, will give the same finish as a brass brush, but with less effort. Fraizers and burrs are made of steel, or carborundum, and are also attached to a pendant drill. They come in many shapes and sizes and can be used to create varying textural finishes – grainy, swirls or matt – depending upon the movement of your wrist and the texture of the fraizer or burr.

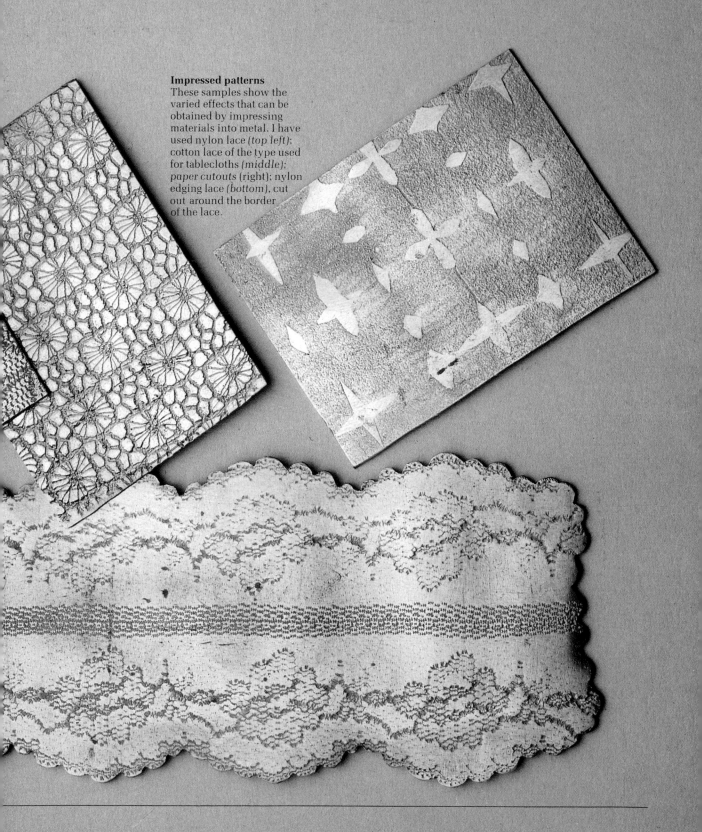

**Impressed patterns**
These samples show the varied effects that can be obtained by impressing materials into metal. I have used nylon lace *(top left)*; cotton lace of the type used for tablecloths *(middle)*; *paper cutouts* (right); nylon edging lace *(bottom)*, cut out around the border of the lace.

# Texturing metal surfaces/2

### Burnishing

Burnishers are made from hard, highly polished steel and have tips of varying sizes. Burnishing produces a smooth, highly polished finish, without removing any of the metal's surface. You can burnish the entire surface of your piece or, alternatively, just the edges. Burnishing not only polishes the edges, but also smooths and hardens them, thus ensuring an extremely durable finish.

Achieving a successful overall burnish will require practice. Systematically rub the burnisher over the area to be polished. To produce a uniform shine, each stroke should blend with the area covered by the previous stroke. If you are polishing a large area you should lubricate the surface with soapy water. To create a textural, rather than a smooth finish, use crosswise or wavy strokes. It is important to look after your burnishers by keeping them clean and by polishing them with very fine emery paper and a metal polish rub.

### Sandblasting

A textured, matt finish can be obtained by sandblasting. This involves using a sandblasting machine, which is an expensive item of equipment. It is advisable, therefore, to take your pieces to a professional polisher. You can create patterns from a mixture of matt and polished areas by covering the high-polish areas with stopout (see below) before the sandblasting. This finish is particularly effective when used on gold and silver.

### Etching

Etching is a means of decorating metal by applying acid. In jewellery making, etching is used for several purposes: making openwork designs with a slightly wavy edging; forming cells for inlaying enamel, wood or resin and creating intricate surface patterns.

### Cleaning

Etching is not a difficult process, but it does require careful attention to detail. The first step is to clean the metal thoroughly. If the metal is not completely clean, the stopout, or acid resist, will not adhere to the surface. Rub the area which is to be protected from the acid with a fine abrasive, such as pumice, or whiting, which has been mixed with household ammonia. Rinse with clean water and dry with a paper towel.

### Acid resist or stopout

There are several resists, or stopouts, which protect metals from the acid solution. The most common of these is 'hard ground' – a mixture of asphaltum, pitch and wax – which can be bought ready mixed. Paint, or dab, this mixture on to the object which is to be etched, making sure that it is completely covered. It is particularly important to cover solder joins, as contact with acid will weaken them considerably.

Lacquermit stopout and tuolene are rubber-based stopouts, generally used for electroplating, which are best applied with a paintbrush.

Less common resists include mixtures of asphaltum, beeswax, mastic gum, pitch, resin, tallow, turpentine and white wax.

Resist pens are ideal for light, fast etching. They are used to draw fine lines of resist on the surface of the metal. Before placing the piece of jewellery in an etching solution, it should be baked to fix the resist. Resist pens are available from electronic and radio components store.

---

### SAFETY PRECAUTIONS

1. Always work near running water.
2. If you get acid on your skin, immediately wash the area with water.
3. If any acid gets into your eyes, flush them with cold water for at least five minutes and then go straight to a doctor.
4. Work by an open window or under an extractor fan.
5. Wear a protective overall and rubber gloves.
6. Keep all food and drink away from your work area.
7. Store acids in tightly sealed containers, out of the reach of children and animals.
8. Keep soda crystals in stock, as they are alkaline and can be used to neutralize acids.
9. Always add acid to water. Never add water to acid.

---

### ACIDS USED FOR ETCHING

It is essential to handle all acids with extreme care. Aside from the general safety precautions already mentioned, there are several golden rules you should observe:
1. Always work with acids that have been diluted with water.
2. Always add acid to water. Never add water to acid.
3. Never pour the acid solution into a metal dish; use a strong oven-proof glass dish instead.
4. If the acid solution has to be heated in order to accelerate the etching process, it is important that the solution is never overheated, as it will produce dangerous fumes.
5. Agitation or movement will also increase the speed of etching. A feather is the ideal tool for gently brushing the surface of the object while it is immersed in the solution, but take care not to slop any of the solution over the edges of the container and only use the feather for a few moments at a time.

---

Draw your design on to tracing paper, tape it into position and then score the design into the resist with a scriber, or any other sharp object. Alternatively, the design may be drawn directly on to the pitch with a pencil.

Depending on the nature of the design, etching may be done before the piece is soldered together, or afterwards. Remember that if etching is done after soldering, all joins must be covered with resist or they will weaken. Carefully mix the acid solution, using the proportions shown in the table. Your basic unit of measurement will depend on the size of the piece to be etched. Hydrofluroic acid, used to etch titanium, is dangerous and highly corrosive. Do not use it unless you have a proper fume cupboard and previous experience in handling dangerous chemicals; take any titanium you wish to have etched to a professional.

Lower the piece gently into the acid solution, using tongs. As soon as your design becomes completely visible, remove the piece from the acid and plunge it into a dish of water. The water dish should be next to the acid dish, so that you do not drip any acid. The piece should then be held under running water until you are sure that all the acid has been washed off.

Asphaltum-based resist is removed by immersing the piece in turpentine, or by rubbing it with a cloth which has been soaked with turpentine. Paint thinner will also remove asphaltum resist, while rubber-based stopouts are removed with Xylene. Wash and dry. Additional finishing touches may include oxidization, which accentuates the etched design, or filling deep etching with acrylic resin or enamel.

## ACID SOLUTIONS FOR USE WITH PARTICULAR METALS

| Metal | Mixture | Proportions | |
|-------|---------|-------------|---|
| Gold | Nitric acid<br>Hydrochloric acid<br>Water | 1<br>3<br>40 | |
| Silver | Nitric acid<br>Water | 1-3<br>1-4 | weak or strong |
| Copper or brass | Sulphuric acid<br>Water | 1<br>2 | strong etch |
| Copper or brass | Hydrochloric acid<br>Potassium chloride<br>Water | 1<br>0.5<br>10 | weak etch |
| Brass | Ferric chloride<br>Water | 2<br>1 | warm |
| Nickel silver | Nitric acid<br>Hydrochloric acid<br>Water | 1<br>3<br>1 | |
| Steel and iron | Hydrochloric acid<br>Water | 1<br>1 | strong etch |
| Pewter | Nitric acid<br>Water | 1<br>4 | |
| Titanium | Hydrofluroic acid<br>Nitric acid<br>Distilled water | 1<br>1<br>10 | see warning |

# Texturing metal surfaces/3

### Advanced etching

These techniques are very specialized and require extra equipment; however, if you enjoy etching, you may wish to explore them. Photographs can be transferred on to metal in etched form by a process known as photo-etching. Spray etching, which is done with a special machine, produces a very accurate pattern, uniform in depth and less apt to get under the surface of the resist.

### Stamping

Stamping is a commercial process, using steel dies, which reproduces identical shapes, or textures and decorates metal. This is an essential labour-saving device, but the quality of the stamping will inevitably vary according to the quality of the original die.

On a smaller scale, hand-driven fly presses can be used to stamp out a limited number of identical shapes or patterns. Most designers will find it cheaper and easier to have their stamping done professionally. However, if you specialize in aluminium or titanium jewellery, it is probably worth investing in a fly press. As sawing these metals is extremely time-consuming, a fly press will enable you to work faster and more efficiently.

### Embossing

Embossing is a means of forcing out designs and shapes with a stamping punch, or a die. The punch can be a simple doming tool which is used to produce a bobble design or its tip can be carved into a design. This, however, is intricate and skilled work.

The metal to be embossed must be thin and well annealed (see p. 45). Place the metal on a leather block, a softwood block or pitch, right side down. Position the punch and hammer it down to the required depth, taking care not to split the metal. For larger areas of metal, carve your design into an old hammer and strike the design directly into the metal surface.

### Impressing

Patterns can be impressed on metal with stamping punches or by using a rolling mill. You can buy impressing tools with readymade commercial designs, commission a craftsman to make tools which incorporate your designs or learn to make your own tools.

A rolling mill will enable you to impress the patterns of materials, such as lace, paper cutouts, copper mesh and dried leaves, on to metal sheet (see pp.142-5). The metal must be fully annealed before it is rolled through the mill. The machine itself should always be well oiled and you should never use too much pressure as this may damage the mechanism.

**Bangles, brooch and earrings
by Ceri Evans**
Unusual effects can often be
obtained by using a simple,
but ingenious, technique.
These pieces have been made
in copper and then covered
with thin, scrunched
peweter.

# Making impressed patterns/1

Attractively patterned jewellery can be created by impressing textural materials, such as lace, mesh and cut-out paper, on to soft metal with a rolling mill. Because this is an expensive piece of equipment you may prefer to ask a professional jeweller to do it for you, but it is important to understand the principles. I have used lace and 1mm thick copper sheet to make these earrings, since it is advisable to practise before you try using silver. The decorative edging is made of silver gallery strip, which you can buy from a jewellery supply store. I have chosen one that resembles lace edging as this best suits the main pattern.

**1 Making earrings with an impressed pattern** Cut a strip of copper narrow enough to fit through the mill. Anneal and pickle (see p. 45).Cut a piece of lace to the same size as the copper strip and lay it on top. Roll them through the mill at maximum pressure. Experiment with different lace types, as some give more attractive patterns. ▶

**2** Make a cardboard template of your earrings, which, in this case, are four triangular shapes with rounded bottoms. Select a suitable area of imprinted metal, attach the template to it and, using a pointed tool, score the outline on to the metal. Cut along the marked edges and then bevel them. Anneal (see p.45) the metal and hammer flat. ▲

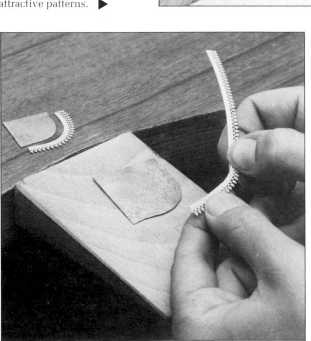

**3** Anneal the gallery strip and bend it with your fingers until it fits around the curved bottoms of the copper shapes. If the strip begins to buckle, hammer it flat. Cut to the exact length required. ◀

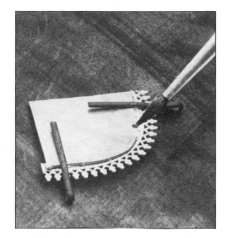

**4** Fix gallery strip to the bottom of each copper shape with cotter pins. The strip should overlap the edge of the copper; it must also lie flat or your soldering will be unsuccessful. Place hard silver solder along the join between the copper and the strip. The solder must be on the back of the earring, so that it does not show. ▲

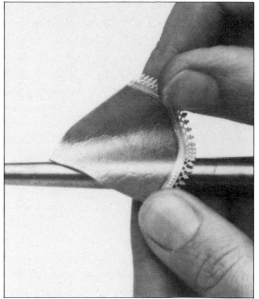

**5** To form waves, anneal each section of the earring and bend it gently around a mandrel with your fingers. If the copper sheet and gallery strip were not completely flat before you soldered them together, you may find that your soldering springs open. ◀

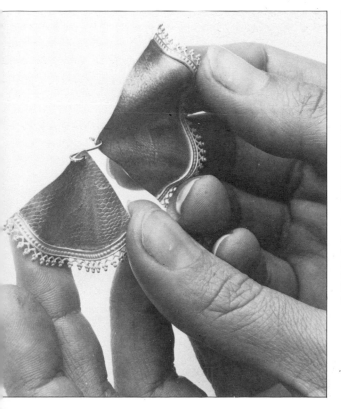

**6** Make an 'S' link of copper or silver wire, just over 1cm in length. Loop each end with round-nosed pliers. Drill a hole in the top corner of each earring piece, link them together and then solder the 'S' link closed. ◀

**7** Thread a small silver bead on a length of copper wire and attach the wire to the top end of the 'S' link with round-nosed pliers. Snip the wire to a suitable length and link it to an earring attachment. Trim and file all the edges. ▲

# Making impressed patterns/2

The twin bangles have been impressed with a wide piece of lace; I have also soldered little flower stampings to the design before having the bangle silver plated and oxidized. The design of the other bangle is based on a piece of *broderie anglaise*, decorated with shell stampings and small domes, gold plated and polished.

Burnish the copper edging and then give the earrings a final all-over polish with an impregnated jeweller's cloth. To emphasize the pattern and texture of the earrings, the impressed areas have been oxidized; while the gallery strip was stopped out so that it would remain a bright silver.

## IMPRESSED BANGLE

Bangles are particularly suited to lace patterning, though other items of jewellery can be decorated by using this technique. Run the metal and lace through the rolling mill, as before. Pierce out the bangle, following the actual shape of the lace edging. Anneal the copper and bend it around a bangle stake to form a simple bangle. Finish by colouring, oxidizing or simply polishing.

# Cloak brooch

The black and white colour scheme of this cloak brooch can be varied by using a brass base or by choosing coloured stones for decoration.

You will need two faceted 15mm clear quartz, 16 4mm spheres of jet, or black rhinestones, eight white crystal teardrops, bought settings for each stone, 1mm thick silver sheet, 9 x 4.5cm in size, 40cm of 2mm silver wire, jump rings, brooch fittings, silver pin wire and assorted silver chains. I have used Prince of Wales chain, rope chain and foxtail chain, but any good quality chain can be used, as long as it fits in with the overall design.

**1 Making a cloak brooch**
Anneal the wire (see p.45) and then bend it into eight curves of equal length. Make a wire frame (see pp.116-9). File the wire at an acute angle to form a square with convex sides. Solder together and pickle (see p.45). Solder the frame to the sheet and pickle. Cut out the shape. Solder a jump ring to the tip. File the edges smooth. ▶

**2** Pierce out a small hole in the centre of the shape to allow light to shine through the quartz. Texture the inner area with a thin glass brush (see p.136), keeping the brush away from the wire frame. Using medium silver solder, solder the central setting in position, followed by the smaller settings. Make sure that the settings remain in position during soldering. Pickle. ▲

**3** Rub the back with emery paper until it is flat and smooth. Solder the brooch fittings to the back with easyflow solder. If a piece requires several solderings, you can protect the joins as you progress from stage to stage by painting them with a paste of powdered rouge and water. Alternatively, you can secure your work with binding wire. ◀

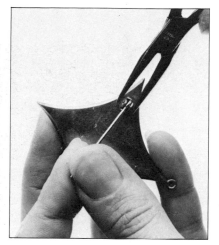

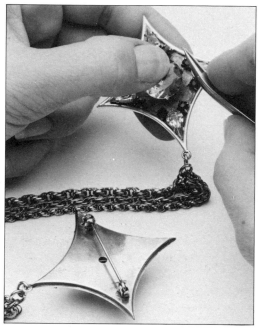

**4** I have used brooch fittings with a 'squeeze action' hinge. Insert the pin wire into the hinge and, using all-purpose pliers, squeeze the fitting until the pin is secured. File the tip of the pin to a point and polish. ▲

**5** I have used three weights of chain so that the loops will hang evenly between the brooch pieces. Oxidize the chains and use two jump rings to attach them to each brooch piece. Clean the edges before applying stopout (see p.139) and oxidize. Set all the stones by pushing over the claws until they hold the stones firmly. Buff the silver with a jeweller's cloth impregnated with polish. ◄

The finished piece can be worn pinned from shoulder to shoulder, forming a necklace, or as a fastening for a cloak or evening jacket.

# Hallmarks

Gold, silver and platinum are not often used in their pure state, therefore they are alloyed with base metals to harden them. Various legal standards regulate the amount of base metal which can be added. The only reliable indication of the quality of the metal used to make an item of jewellery is the hallmark.

A hallmark is a series of marks punched into the metal certifying that an item has been assayed and that the gold, silver and platinum content is up to standard. The word hallmark is derived from Goldsmiths Hall which was the original Assay Office in London.

The system of hallmarking used in Britain began in 1300 with the marking of gold and silver items. This early Act defined the standards of fineness for gold and silver and introduced the king's mark, which later became the Assay Office mark – a leopard's head for London. Later an anchor became the symbol for Birmingham, a crown for Sheffield (replaced by a rose in 1904) and a castle for Edinburgh.

In 1363 a second mark – the maker's mark became compulsory. Initially this would have been a decorative device, but it then became the initials of the maker.

The practice of using a letter of the alphabet to show which year the item was submitted for assay began in 1478. The letter system is very complicated, but it enables a hallmarked item to be dated exactly.

The standard mark indicates the purity of the metal. There are four standards of gold in this country – 9, 14, 18 and 22 carat. Figures in a shield shape denote the percentage of gold in the alloy. The percentage of silver is denoted by distinguishing pictorial marks.

In 1975 the hallmarking of platinum became a legal requirement. Alloys below 950 parts per thousand may not be described as platinum.

In 1976 an International Convention drew up a system of internationally recognized hallmarks which have been agreed upon by Austria, Finland, Ireland, Norway, Portugal, Sweden, Switzerland and Britain. In many other countries, including the United States, there is no official system of hallmarking, so the makers usually stamp their own marks in the metal.

If you are making jewellery for your own use, there is no need to have it hallmarked, but items made for commercial purposes should be sent for assaying. On your first visit to an Assay Office you will have to register your maker's mark, which will consist of a frame surrounding your initials. You may choose from an assortment of frames. You are then allowed to take or send your pieces to the nearest Assay Office in a finished, but unpolished state, bearing your maker's mark. If two or more metals have been combined, the piece will be marked for the lower quality only.

| Maker's mark | Standard mark | Assay Office | Date letter |

**Components of a hallmark**
In Britain a hallmark consists of: the maker's mark; the standard mark which defines the precious metal content of the alloy; the Assay Office mark which identifies the particular office where the item was assayed; and the date mark which indicates the year in which the item was hallmarked.

**STANDARD MARK**

| GOLD | | SILVER |
|---|---|---|
| 22 carat (91.66%) | 916 | |
| 18 carat (75.0%) | 750 | Sterling (92.5%) |
| 14 carat (58.5%) | 585 | Britannia (95.8%) |
| 9 carat (37.5%) | 375 | PLATINUM 95.0% |

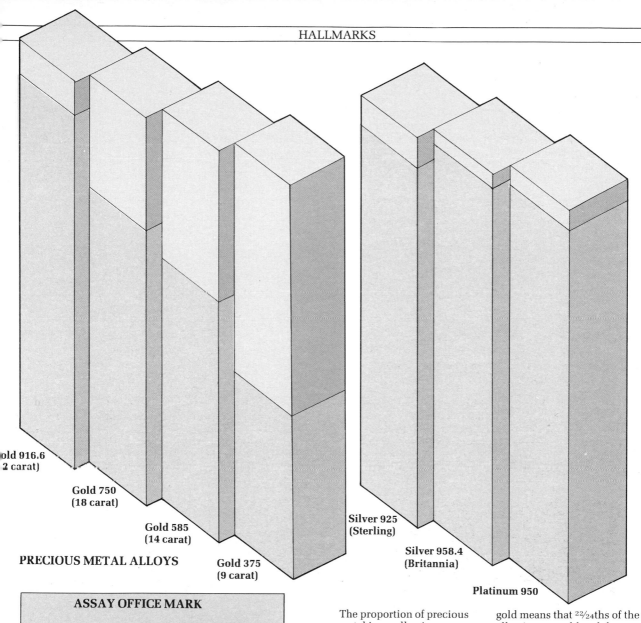

old 916.6
2 carat)

**Gold 750
(18 carat)**

**Gold 585
(14 carat)**

**PRECIOUS METAL ALLOYS**

**Gold 375
(9 carat)**

**Silver 925
(Sterling)**

**Silver 958.4
(Britannia)**

**Platinum 950**

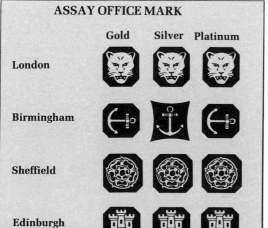

| ASSAY OFFICE MARK | | | |
|---|---|---|---|
| | Gold | Silver | Platinum |
| London | | | |
| Birmingham | | | |
| Sheffield | | | |
| Edinburgh | | | |

The proportion of precious metal in an alloy is now measured in parts per thousand by weight. The previous system for measuring gold was the 'carat'. A carat is $\frac{1}{24}$th part of the whole. Therefore 22 carat gold means that $\frac{22}{24}$ths of the alloy is pure gold and the remainder a base metal.

The Standard mark is an official guarantee that the alloy contains at least the specified proportion of precious metal.

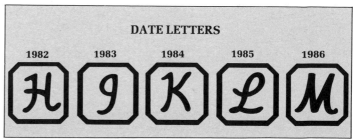

| DATE LETTERS | | | | |
|---|---|---|---|---|
| 1982 | 1983 | 1984 | 1985 | 1986 |
| H | I | K | L | M |

# Charts and tables/1

**Gauges** When you first start making jewellery it is best to order wire and sheet metal in millimetres. This is because there is no single standard of gauge measurement in Britain and different companies tend to use different systems. The system most often used is the Birmingham Metal Gauge (BMG), but there are several others, including the Brown and Sharpe (B. & S.) wire gauge which is the standard gauge for wire and sheet metal in the United States. It is important, therefore, to find out which gauge is used by your regular suppliers.

## GAUGES<br>THE BROWN AND SHARPE WIRE GAUGE

| Number of gauge | Inches | Millimetres |
|---|---|---|
| 6/0 | 0.580 | 14.73 |
| 5/0 | 0.5165 | 13.119 |
| 4/0 | 0.46 | 11.68 |
| 3/0 | 0.409 | 10.388 |
| 2/0 | 0.364 | 9.24 |
| 1/0 | 0.324 | 8.23 |
| 1 | 0.289 | 7.338 |
| 2 | 0.257 | 6.527 |
| 3 | 0.229 | 5.808 |
| 4 | 0.204 | 5.18 |
| 5 | 0.181 | 4.59 |
| 6 | 0.162 | 4.11 |
| 7 | 0.144 | 3.66 |
| 8 | 0.128 | 3.24 |
| 9 | 0.114 | 2.89 |
| 10 | 0.101 | 2.565 |
| 11 | 0.090 | 2.28 |
| 12 | 0.080 | 2.03 |
| 13 | 0.071 | 1.79 |
| 14 | 0.064 | 1.625 |
| 15 | 0.057 | 1.447 |
| 16 | 0.050 | 1.27 |
| 17 | 0.045 | 1.14 |
| 18 | 0.040 | 1.016 |
| 19 | 0.035 | 0.889 |
| 20 | 0.031 | 0.787 |
| 21 | 0.028 | 0.711 |
| 22 | 0.025 | 0.635 |
| 23 | 0.022 | 0.558 |
| 24 | 0.020 | 0.508 |
| 25 | 0.017 | 0.431 |
| 26 | 0.015 | 0.381 |
| 27 | 0.0148 | 0.376 |
| 28 | 0.012 | 0.304 |
| 29 | 0.0116 | 0.29 |
| 30 | 0.01 | 0.254 |
| 31 | 0.008 | 0.203 |
| 32 | 0.0079 | 0.199 |
| 33 | 0.007 | 0.177 |
| 34 | 0.006 | 0.152 |
| 35 | 0.0055 | 0.142 |
| 36 | 0.005 | 0.127 |

## THE MELTING POINTS OF VARIOUS METALS

| Metal – in pure form | Centigrade | Fahrenheit |
|---|---|---|
| Aluminium | 659.7 | 1219.6 |
| Brass | 1015 | 1859 |
| Copper | 1083 | 1981.4 |
| Gold | 1063 | 1945.4 |
| Iron | 1535 | 2795 |
| Lead | 327.4 | 621.32 |
| Nickel | 1455 | 2619 |
| Platinum | 1773.5 | 3192.3 |
| Silver | 960.5 | 1728.9 |
| Steel | 1350 | 2430 |
| Tin | 231.89 | 417.5 |
| Titanium | 1668 | 3035 |
| Zinc | 419.47 | 755.04 |

## JUDGING TEMPERATURES BY COLOUR

| Colour | Centigrade | Fahrenheit |
|---|---|---|
| Red heat, visible in dark | 400 | 752 |
| Red heat, visible in twilight | 474 | 885 |
| Red heat, visible in daylight | 525 | 975 |
| Red heat, visible in sunlight | 581 | 1077 |
| Dark red | 700 | 1292 |
| Dull cherry red | 800 | 1472 |
| Cherry red | 900 | 1652 |
| Bright cherry red | 1000 | 1832 |
| Orange-red | 1100 | 2012 |
| Orange-yellow | 1200 | 2192 |
| Yellow-white | 1300 | 2372 |
| White welding heat | 1400 | 2552 |
| Brilliant white | 1500 | 2732 |
| Dazzling white, blue-white | 1600 | 2912 |

See chart on p152 for abbreviations

## BIRMINGHAM METAL GAUGE    ROUND WIRE AND SHEET METAL

| BMG | Inches | Millimetres | Lgth per oz silver | Silver | Wts in oz t 9ct gold | 18ct gold |
|---|---|---|---|---|---|---|
| 8 | 0.021 | 0.55 | 42ft | 0.024ft | 0.035ft | 0.0395ft |
| 10 | 0.027 | 0.70 | 27ft | 0.038ft | 0.051ft | 0.066ft |
| 11 | 0.031 | 0.80 | 19½ft | 0.052ft | 0.068ft | 0.089ft |
| 12 | 0.036 | 0.90 | 16ft | 0.064ft | 0.079ft | 0.104ft |
| 14 | 0.042 | 1.00 | 9¾ft | 0.102ft | 0.114ft | 0.130ft |
| 16 | 0.051 | 1.25 | 7½ft | 0.133ft | 0.147ft | 0.203ft |
| 18 | 0.060 | 1.50 | 5½ft | 0.192ft | 0.240ft | 0.316ft |
| 20 | 0.065 | 1.65 | 4¾ft | 0.211ft | 0.266ft | 0.348ft |
| 22 | 0.072 | 1.85 | 3½ft | 0.282ft | 0.355ft | 0.466ft |
| 24 | 0.086 | 2.00 | 2½ft | 0.420ft | 0.516ft | 0.674ft |
| 26 | 0.104 | 2.50 | 1¾ft | 0.610ft | 0.760ft | 0.996ft |
| 28 | 0.125 | 3.00 | 15in | 0.850ft | 1.066ft | 1.400ft |
| 30 | 0.150 | 4.00 | 9½in | 1.252ft | 1.62ft | 2.124ft |
| 32 | 0.187 | 5.00 | 6¾in | 0.148in | 0.184in | 0.2in |
| 36 | 0.250 | 6.40 | 4in | 0.262in | 0.331in | 0.433in |
| ⅜in | 0.375 | 9.50 | 1⅝in | 0.600in | 0.744in | 0.978in |
| ½in | 0.500 | 12.80 | 11in | 1.042in | 1.250in | 1.730in |

## HALF ROUND HIGH WIRE (HEIGHT ½ DEPTH OF BASE

| BMG | Inches | Millimetres | Lgth per oz silver | Silver | Wts in oz t 9ct gold | 18ct gold |
|---|---|---|---|---|---|---|
| 20 | 0.062 | 1.5 | 11ft | 0.098ft | 0.121ft | 0.156ft |
| 25 | 0.092 | 2.3 | 3¼ft | 0.314ft | 0.392ft | 0.516ft |
| 28 | 0.125 | 3 | 2½ft | 0.404ft | 0.502ft | 0.658ft |
| 30 | 0.155 | 4 | 1½ft | 0.660ft | 0.838ft | 1.100ft |
| 32 | 0.187 | 4.8 | 12½ft | 0.083in | 0.102in | 0.136in |
| 36 | 0.250 | 6.4 | 7¾in | 0.132in | 0.166in | 0.218in |

## HALF ROUND SHALLOW WIRE

| BMG | Inches | Millimetres | Lgth per oz silver | Silver | Wts in oz t 9ct gold | 18ct gold |
|---|---|---|---|---|---|---|
| 24 | 0.080 x 0.046 | 2.00 x 1 | 5ft | 0.193ft | 0.210ft | 0.228ft |
| 25 | 0.096 x 0.036 | 2.3 x 0.9 | 7ft | 0.147ft | 0.183ft | 0.237ft |
| 28 | 0.120 x 0.042 | 3.00 x 1 | 4¼ft | 0.236ft | 0.252ft | 0.332ft |
| 30 | 0.155 x 0.046 | 4.00 x 1.1 | 3⅓ft | 0.300ft | 0.324ft | 0.476ft |
| 32 | 0.187 x 0.060 | 4.8 x 1.5 | 2ft | 0.522ft | 0.552ft | 0.860ft |
| 36 | 0.250 x 0.082 | 6.4 x 2 | 12½in | 0.080in | 0.099in | 0.131in |
| ⁵⁄₁₆ | 0.312 x 0.086 | 7.8 x 2.2 | 4¾in | 0.210in | 0.267in | 0.350in |
| ⅜ | 0.375 x 0.125 | 9.5 x 3 | 4½in | 0.217in | 0.270in | 0.354in |
| ½ | 0.500 x 0.125 | 12.7 x 3 | 3½in | 0.281in | 0.350in | 0.465in |

# Charts and tables/2

## BUYING METALS AND SOLDERS

Most precious metal dealers will be able to supply the following types of metal and solders:

9ct Yellow Sheet and Wire
9ct Hard Yellow Sheet and Wire
9ct Enamelling Sheet and Wire
9ct White Sheet and Wire/Medium/Hard
9ct Red Sheet and Wire
9ct Green Sheet and Wire
14ct Yellow and Red Sheet and Wire
18ct Yellow Sheet, Wire and Casting
18ct Yellow Sheet and Wire Hard
18ct Green Sheet and Wire
18ct White in Medium/Soft/Hard Sheet and Wire
20ct Yellow and Red Sheet and Wire
22ct Yellow and Red Sheet and Wire
Pure Gold Sheet and Wire
Platinum Sheet and Wire
Gold Wire/Hard/Pure
Palladium Sheet and Wire
Gold Wire/Pure

Solder in Platinum, Gold and Silver Hard/Medium/Easy/X Easy

Various fluxes

Polishing products

## CONVERSION FACTORS

To convert feet per Troy oz to cm per Gram multiply by 0.980

To convert inches per Troy oz to cm per Gram multiply by 0.0816

To convert Troy oz per foot to Grams per cm multiply by 1.02

To convert Troy oz per inch to Grams per cm multiply by 12.24

## ROUND WIRE ON 1 OZ REELS

Available in Fine Silver, Sterling Silver, 9ct Gold

| BMG | Inches | Millimetres | Approx. length sterling silver |
|-----|--------|-------------|-------------------------------|
| 1 | 008 | 0.2 | 500ft |
| 4 | 012 | 0.3 | 166ft |
| 6 | 016 | 0.4 | 90ft |

## STANDARD ABBREVIATIONS

| | |
|---|---|
| cg | centigrams |
| cir. | circumference |
| c.p. | chemically pure |
| cm | centimetre |
| ct | carat |
| cwt | hundredweight |
| deg | degree |
| dm | decimetre |
| dr | dram |
| dwt | pennyweight (troy) |
| fl oz | fluid ounces |
| ft | foot |
| g | gram |
| gal | gallon |
| gr | grains |
| hr | hour |
| ID | inside diameter |
| in | inch |
| kg | kilogram |
| l | litre |
| lb | pound |
| lb av | pound avoirdupois |
| lb t | pound troy |
| m | metre |
| mg | milligram |
| ml | millilitre |
| mm | millimetre |
| OD | outside diameter |
| o.f. | oxidizing flame |
| oz | ounce |
| oz ap | ounces apothecary weight |
| oz t | ounces troy |
| pt | pint |
| p.s. | pearl size |
| psi | pounds per square inch |
| qt | quart |
| r.f. | reducing flame |
| rpm | revolutions per minute |
| rps | revolutions per second |
| s.s. | stone size |
| yd | yard |
| wt | weight |

## RECIPES FOR COLOURING METAL

| Material | Chemicals | Quantity | Method |
|---|---|---|---|
| **Copper** **Reddish bronze** **to dark brown** | Sodium hydroxide Sulphurated potash Water | 85g 56g 4.5l | Add the sodium hydroxide and sulphurated potash to the water. Use a heat-resistant glass dish and heat to 76°C. Attach the piece of jewellery to a piece of copper or brass wire and immerse the jewellery in the solution. Allow the solution to cool and remove the piece as soon as you are satisfied with the colour. Rinse, and then fix the colour with lacquer, or fixative. |
| **Brass and copper** **Antique greeny-yellow** | Copper nitrate Ammonium chloride Calcium chloride Water | 113g 113g 113g 4.5l | You can paint the solution on to the metal; alternatively, you can immerse the piece of jewellery in the solution. When the colour appears, remove the piece and boil it in water. Allow it to dry naturally. To intensify the colour, repeat this process. Fix the colour with lacquer, or fixative. |
| **Brass** **Antique green** | Nickel ammonium sulphate Sodium thiosulphate Water | 227g 227g 4.5l | Put the solution in a heat-resistant glass dish and heat to 71°C. Immerse the piece of jewellery in the solution. Alternatively, you can stipple colour on to the surface with a brush. Rinse, and fix the colour with lacquer, or fixative. |
| **Brass** **Blue-black** | Copper carbonate Ammonia Water | 113g 0.6l 1.4l | Mix the ammonia and the copper carbonate together and add the mixture to the water. Heat the solution to 79°C and immerse the piece of jewellery. Allow the solution to cool. Remove the piece and fix the colour by dipping it into a 2½% caustic soda solution. |
| **Brass** **Blue** | Lead acetate Sodium thiosulphate Acetic acid Water | 56-113g 226g 113g 4.5l | Heat the solution to 82°C and use the same method as for colouring brass (above). However, the colour is fixed with lacquer, or a fixative. |
| **Brass** **Yellow to bright red** | Copper carbonate Caustic soda Water | 2 parts 1 part 10 parts | Mix the ingredients and immerse the piece of jewellery until the surface has changed to the required colour. Rinse, and then fix the colour with lacquer, or fixative. |
| **Brass and copper** **Turquoise** | Acetic acid | ½ cup | Pour the acetic acid into a plastic container with a lid. The piece of jewellery should either be placed on a copper mesh support, or it can be suspended with wire. Tightly secure the lid. Because the colour change is induced by the acid fumes, it is essential that the lid fits properly. Leave the piece of jewellery in the container for approximately 48 hours. Allow it to dry and then fix the colour with lacquer, or fixative. |

153

# Glossary

**Acrylic resin** See *polyester resin*

**Alloy** Metallic substance formed by the combination of two or more metals.

**Alum** An acid-free pickle *(see pickle)*.

**Amber** A translucent fossil resin – its colour ranges from pale yellow through to deep orange.

**Annealing** The process of heating metal and then allowing it to cool in order to make it soft enough to work effectively.

**Anode** A positive electrode or terminal.

**Anodizing** An electrochemical process that deposits a controllable coating of oxide on the surface of certain metals, producing coloration.

**Appliqué** Attached to the surface.

**Asbestos block** This is used as a base for the soldering area to protect the workbench. Synthetic asbestos blocks are now made as an alternative.

**Assay** An accurate measurement of the platinum, gold or silver content of an item by an official Assay Office.

**Baroque pearl** Irregular or misshapen pearl.

**Base metal** Any non-ferrous metal other than gold or silver.

**Basse-taille** A more refined form of champlevé *(see champlevé)* in which a graded colour effect is achieved by varying the depth of cut in the metal.

**Bezel** The ledge, or base, of a setting. The girdle *(see girdle)* of the stone rests on this base.

**Binding wire** Steel wire which is used to bind two pieces of metal together during soldering *(see soldering)*.

**Borax** A flux used to assist in the soldering process. It can be bought as a powder, in lump form, or in a compressed cone.

**Burnishing** Method of polishing by smoothing and rubbing a metallic surface with a steel burnisher.

**Butterfly attachment** A means of securing an earring for pierced ears. It is a strip of metal, with a hole the diameter of the earring rod drilled in its centre and its ends turned up into scrolls which grip the rod tightly, keeping the earring in place.

**Cabochon cut** A smooth, dome-shaped cut with no facets.

**Carat** (1) A measure of the purity of gold. (2) A unit of weight used for gemstones.

**Carborundum** A type of abrasive stone used to sharpen tools and smooth surfaces.

**Casting** Technique used to reproduce replicas of an original.

**Champlevé** A method of enamelling in which the design is carved into the surface of a metal object and enamel is poured into the recesses.

**Chasing** The technique of punching a relief design in metal from the front.

**Cire perdue** Lost wax casting – a method of casting using wax and plaster.

**Cloisonné** A method of enamelling in which little cells made of wire are filled with enamel.

**Cloisons** Cells on the surface of a piece of goldwork, formed by soldering walls on to a back plate.

**Collet** The area of a setting into which a stone is placed.

**Composite stone** A simulation of a gemstone made by joining two pieces of stone together. One of these is usually an inferior material. This is done to provide a better colour or a harder wearing surface.

**Doming** A technique for making circular depressions in annealed metal, using a block and punch.

**Draw plate** A steel plate with holes of varying shapes and sizes for reducing the thickness, or changing the shape, of wire.

**Ductile** A quality in certain metals that enables them to be bent or reshaped.

**Electroforming** The process of producing an object by depositing layers of metal on to a mould with a conductive surface by applying an electric current. The thickness of the layers is consistent and controllable.

**Electroplating** The process of depositing a layer of metal on to a conductive surface through the use of DC current.

**Embossing** A technique of stamping patterns on to the surface of metals.

**Emery paper** Paper with an abrasive surface, used for removing scratches and smoothing rough surfaces. It is available in a number of grades.

**Enamel** A technique of fusing coloured glass to metal.

**Engraving** The technique of cutting figures, patterns or letters into metal or other hard surfaces.

**Etching** A technique of decorating metal by a controlled application of acid.

**Facet** A flat surface produced on a cut diamond or other precious stone to enhance its brilliance and colour.

**Ferrous** Metals that contain iron.

**Filigree** Ornamental work in very fine wire, often as decoration soldered to a sheet metal base.

**Findings** Jewellery components such as links, catches and fastenings.

**Fire stain** The black coating of copper oxide which forms on silver when it is over-heated.

**Flux** A substance which keeps the surface of a metal free from oxidization during soldering and which also assists the flow of the solder. Borax is the flux most commonly used *(see borax)*.

**Foil** Term used to describe metal that is so thin that it can be folded, twisted, etc. without annealing.

**Foiled stone** Stones with a poor, or a pale, colour are often mounted in a closed setting and the back of the stone foiled with a suitable coloured paper.

**Forging** Hammering annealed metal to change its shape.

**Gallery strip** Decorated strip of metal, usually stamped out, used for decoration.

**Gilding** The process of applying a thin layer of gold to another material using heat or glue to bond them together.

**Girdle** The widest circumference of a gemstone.

**Grain** A tiny ball of metal (see granulation).

**Granulation** The decoration of a metal surface by the application of tiny grains of gold or silver.

**Hallmark** Stamp which indicates the quality of precious metals.

**Ingot** A bar of metal.

**Inlaying** The technique of embedding one material flush into the surface of another.

**Intaglio** An object with a hollowed out design – usually a gemstone but sometimes metal.

**Investment plaster** A finely ground plaster that is able to withstand very high temperatures without cracking. It is used to make moulds for casting.

**Jet** A fossil wood of an intense black colour which can be highly polished. It was particularly popular in Victorian times for use in mourning jewellery.

**Lapidary** A cutter, polisher and engraver of gemstones.

**Leafing** Very thin sheets of gold or silver, used mostly in bookbinding, but also in jewellery making.

**Lost wax casting** (see cire perdue).

**Malleability** The property of being easily shaped without cracking.

**Mandrel** A shape, usually made from wood or steel, for curving metal.

**Mill** Piece of equipment used for flattening sheet metal.

**Niello** A technique developed by the Romans which is similar to enamel. It is a black compound made from a mixture of metal and sulphur.

**Non-ferrous** Metal which does not contain iron.

**Obsidian** A dark vitreous lava.

**Oxidization** A natural process, which occurs as metal is exposed to air and moisture. It can also be induced, by using heat or chemicals, to create surface coloration.

**Paillon** Solder generally comes in strip form which is then cut into extremely small pieces called paillons.

**Paste** A brilliant glass with a high lead content used to make imitation gemstones.

**Pavé** A type of setting in which many small stones are grouped closely together.

**Pickle** A chemical solution, containing acid, used to clean oxides and flux (see flux) off metals after annealing or soldering.

**Piercing** Cutting out a pattern in sheet metal or any other material.

**Plique-à-jour** Openwork filled with enamel. The cells have no backs so that the light can shine through as in a stained glass window.

**Polyester resin** A plastic in liquid form which becomes solid when mixed with a setting catalyst.

**Quenching** After metal has been heated during the process of annealing, it can be cooled quickly with water.

**Refractory** Metals that are hard to melt or to shape.

**Repoussé** A relief design punched into metal from the back.

**Rouge** A fine red polish used in the final polishing stages of metal. It is available in block or powder form.

**Shank** The part of a ring that encircles the finger.

**Soldering** The technique of joining two pieces of metal together by flowing molten metal between them which, on cooling, unites them. Solders consist of a specific metal, such as gold or silver, and a proportion of a baser metal.

**Solitaire** A gemstone set on its own.

**Sprue** A channel which allows the passage of molten metal into a casting mould.

**Stamping** The technique of forming a pattern in sheet metal, by hammering a metal tool engraved with a design into the metal surface, or by using a fly press.

**Stopout** (1)A means of creating patterns during electroplating and oxidizing by using a protective rubber coating. (2) A means of protecting metal during etching.

**Tensile strength** The maximum pressure that a metal can withstand during the process of stretching without fracturing.

**Tortoiseshell** This does not come from the tortoise, but from the carapace of the Hawksbill sea turtle. There are artificial substitutes available.

**Triblet** A tapered steel rod for shaping rings.

**Tripoli** A coarse abrasive used in the first stages of polishing metal.

**Troy weight** System of weight measurement used for precious metals before the introduction of the metric system.

**Water of Ayr stone** A type of abrasive stone used in combination with water to smooth enamel or niello surfaces.

**Work hardening** As metal is bent, twisted or shaped it will harden, reducing its workability.

# Index

Page numbers in *italics* refer to illustrations and captions.

## A

abalone shell cufflinks, 110
acids:
    for etching, 138
    safety, 45, 138
acrylic resin, 84
    earrings, 88, 88-9
Adam, Jane, 20
agate, 30, 31
Alhambra Collection, 10, 18-19
aluminium, 41, 125
amber, 30, 33
amethyst, 31
    synthetic, 31
ammonium sulphide, 124-5
annealing, 44-5, 45
anodizing, 125-6
    fixing colours, 126
aquamarine, 31
Assay Offices, 148-9

## B

baisse-taille enamelling, 109
Baker, Martin, 24, 101
banded black onyx, 31
bangles:
    by Ceri Evans, 141
    by Andrew Logan, 26
    by Tom McEwan, 21
    coloured brass, 132,
132-5
    from objets trouvés, 95
    impressed, 144-5
bar brooch, 76, 76-7
barrell polishers, 44
beads, string of, 60, 60-1
Beane, Hilary, 17, 25
bick iron, 39
Binns, Tom, 16, 27, 90, 91, 93
Birmingham Metal Gauge, 150, 151
blood-stone, 31
blow torches, 47
blue goldstone, 30
blue john, 31
blue lace agate, 31
borax cone, 39
Botswana agate, 30
bowls, by Chris Howes, 126
bows, 128, 128-31
boxes:
    by Martin Baker, 24, 101
    glass, 101
brass, 41
Britannia silver, 41
brooches:
    bar, 76, 76-7
    brass, 50, 50-1
    by Jane Adam, 20
    by Martin Baker, 32
    by Hilary Beane, 17, 25
    by Tom Binns, 16, 27, 90, 93
    by Cartier, 28
    by Annabelle Ely, 21
    by Ceri Evans, 141
    by George Fouquet, 105
    by Dinny Hall, 14
    by Fred Riche, 23
    cloak, 146-7
    with crystal decoration, 74, 74-5
    filigree, 80, 80-3
    fittings, 70
    from objets trouvés, 95-7
    Londesborough, 101
Brown and Sharpe Wire Gauge, 150
buffers, 136
buffing brushes, 39

burnishers, 38
burnishing, 138
burrs, 136

## C

cabochon cuts, 33
cabochon settings,
    earrings with, 56, 56-7
    rings with, 58, 58-9
Calder, Alexander, 12
carat, 40
Cartier, 28
cast iron, 42
Castellani, 10
casting, 66-7, 66, 67
    advanced, 67
    cuttlefish, 66
    lost wax, 66
    rubber moulds, 66-7, 67
    simple designs, 68, 68-9
    sprues, 66, 66
catches, 70
centre punches, 39, 44
ceramics, 92
chains, 70, 71
    simple silver, 72, 72-3
champlevé enamelling, 109
chasing, 104
chemicals:
    oxidation, 124
    safety, 37, 45, 84, 124
chromium, 42
citrine, 31
claw setting, 54, 55
cloak brooch, 146, 146-7
cloisonné enamelling, 109
clothes, jewellery and, 11, 12
coiling wire, 79, 79
Cole, Madelaine, 15, 22
collet plate and punch, 39, 54
collets, 54, 55
colour:
    anodizing, 125-6

design and, 13
    enamelling, 106-7
    judging temperatures by, 150
    oxidation, 124-5
    stones, 33
comb, by Madelaine Cole, 22
copper, 41
    oxidation, 124
coral, 33
cornelian, 30, 31
coronet settings, 54
Cowper Jackie, 87, 102
cubic zirconia, 33
cufflinks:
    abalone shell, 110, 110-11
    by Jackie Cowper, 87, 102
cutting stones, 33
cuttlefish casting, 66

## D

decoupage, 92
Derbyshire blue john, 31
design:
    choosing materials, 11
    colour and, 13
    inspiration for, 10
    light and, 12
    principles of, 10-29
    proportion and, 13
    shape and, 13
    techniques and, 11, 13
    weight and, 13
'Detail', 85, 87
diamond, 30, 31
    artificial, 33
dividers, 39
doming, 46, 46
doming blocks, 39
doming punches, 39
draw plates, 78
drawing and sketching, 10
drawing wire, 78

## Acknowledgements

The author and publisher would like to thank the following organizations for their kind help in the production of this book:

The British Museum; Blundells; Charles Cooper; Craft O'Hans; Detail; Exchange Findings; Louis Kaplin Associates; Parks and Young Ltd; The Victoria and Albert Museum.


The author and publisher would also like to thank the following artists who contributed to the book:

Jane Adam; Martin Baker; Hilary Beane; Tom Binns; Jackie Cowper; Madelaine Cole; Annabelle Ely; Tom McEwan; Ceri Evans; Charmian Inman; Chris Howes; Andrew Logan; Fred Riche; Pepe Taylor.

The author would especially like to thank:
Tom Binns for his patience and creative support; Chris Howes for his technical help; Sally and Tony of the Paul Press for putting up with my erratic temperament; Mandy Little for her guidance; June Marsh, Fashion Editor of *Options Magazine* for suggesting that I write this book in the first place; my mother, Susan, for her continual encouragement in whatever I endeavour to do; my father, David, for all his support during the first few years of beginning my own business; Don Wood for the photography and for being such a pleasure to work with; Pepe Taylor for helping me and listening to me while I work; Corinna and Paola for modelling the jewellery; Phillip McCarthy at Barclays Bank; the Jewellery Department at the Central School of Art and Design.